Look at Me
When I Talk to You

ESL Learners in Non-ESL Classrooms

SYLVIA HELMER

CATHERINE EDDY

Pippin

Designed by John Zehethofer
Edited by Dyanne Rivers
Typeset by Jay Tee Graphics Ltd.
Printed and bound in Canada by AGMV Marquis Imprimeur Inc.

We acknowledge the financial support of the Government of Canada
through the Book Publishing Industry Development Program for our
publishing activities.

We acknowledge the support of the Government of Ontario through the
Ontario Media Development Corporation's Ontario Book Initiative.

National Library of Canada Cataloguing in Publication

Helmer, Sylvia, 1948-

Look at me when I talk to you : ESL learners
in non-ESL classrooms / Sylvia Helmer,
Catherine L. Eddy.—2nd ed.

(Pippin teacher's library; 39)
Includes bibliographical references.
ISBN 0-88751-108-2

1. English language—Study and teaching as a second language.
2. Minorities—Education. 3. Communication in education. I. Eddy,
Catherine L., 1947- II. Title. III. Series.

PE1128.A2H453 2003   428'.0071'5   C2003-900850-9

10 9 8 7 6 5 4 3

This book is dedicated to the many ESL learners in whose presence we have had the opportunity to teach—and to learn.

We would like to thank Mary Ashworth for her support andencouragement. In addition, we thank Jodie Johnson, Frank McCormick, Ken MacPherson, Kim Rebane, Rosalie Tully and Gail Wynston for their valuable comments on an earlier version of this manuscript. Finally, Nolan and Lee, our husbands, deserve a large vote of thanks for their enduring patience and support during the many, many hours we spent totally immersed in "the book."

Responsibility for the content is, of course, ours.

CONTENTS

Introduction 7

Setting the Stage 11
Culture 17

Awareness of Culture 20

ESL Learners Are Individuals 26

ESL Learners and Communication 35
Coverbal Communication 36
Nonverbal Communication 39
A Complex Combination 49

ESL Learners and Schooling 50
Instructional Strategies 51
Cultural Conflicts 54
Building Bridges 60

Values and Beliefs 61
Assertiveness—Compliance 63
Dominance—Submission 65
Disclosure—Privacy 71
Direct Communication—Indirect Communication 73
Flexible Time—Time As a Commodity 76
The Core of Our Humanity 79

Putting It All Together 80
A Final Word 94

Resources   *95*

General   *95*
Putting It All Together   *98*
Our Personal Favorites   103

INTRODUCTION

People don't get along
because they fear each other.
People fear each other
because they don't know each other.
They don't know each other
because they have not properly communicated with each
other.

Martin Luther King, Jr.

Culture is complex. Communication is complex. And working with students from a variety of ethnic and cultural backgrounds provides ample evidence that this complexity is greater than the sum of its parts.

This book is intended for teachers of all grade levels who instruct students whose home language is not English and whose cultural backgrounds vary. Various terms have been used to designate these students—English as a second language (ESL), English as an additional language (EAL), limited English proficient (LEP) and English-language learners (ELLs). The term ESL learner, though not necessarily technically correct, will be used throughout this book.

Though many books deal with aspects of culture or communication, this book combines these elements by describing and interpreting scenarios experienced by both elementary and secondary classroom teachers. In writing the book, we hoped to achieve a number of goals, including:

— Assisting classroom teachers in their efforts to work with ESL learners in their classes

— Raising awareness of both cultural differences and similarities, and how these may manifest themselves in everyday schooling situations
— Increasing empathy for and understanding of these similarities and differences among all learners, student and adult
— Posing questions for further exploration

This book will not deal with theories of language acquisition, nor will it deal extensively with the learning styles of specific cultural groups. Though reference may be made to both these issues, we encourage readers to investigate other sources for more detailed information. Some of these are listed in the section of this book titled "Resources."

Whenever teachers work with ESL learners, gaps in communication will arise for a variety of reasons. First, a simple lack of English skills creates the potential for miscommunication. In addition, there are significant differences in the way individuals habitually interact with others, especially when they are from different cultural or ethnic backgrounds.

When these "differences" are associated with second-language learners in any classroom, they can inadvertently reinforce the idea that responsibility for teaching English rests exclusively with the ESL specialist. A typical reaction is: "I'm not a language teacher; I teach math (or music, or science, etc.). Teaching English is the job of the ESL specialist."

But teaching ESL learners is not the exclusive domain of the specialist. Because research in second-language acquisition indicates that it takes an average of five or more years to become fluent in a second language, responsibility for meeting the educational needs of these learners extends far beyond the ESL teacher alone.

We believe that working with and supporting students who are learning English as an additional language is the province of *all* teachers, no matter what their specialty. As a result, examples of differences in culture and communication will be provided throughout the book. The focus of this identification is to raise awareness of and generate questions that will help all teachers explore and examine alternative ways of thinking about how these differences may affect the teaching and learning that happens in their classrooms. The first chapter describes the changes that have occurred in our schools. It also addresses the idea of culture and the reasons we must consider its impact.

Though the second chapter is an invitation to look at culture from several points of view, it focuses on encouraging us to think about our own culture. Any examination of culture must begin with the self.

The third chapter begins to address the question of who "they" are. "They" include all whose first language is not English, and who may be from around the globe.

The next chapter deals with cultural communication systems, with particular emphasis on nonverbal systems, which greatly influence our understanding of communication in general. Aspects of communication such as gestures, tonal emphasis, touching, eye contact and personal space are introduced and discussed.

Issues related to schooling are dealt with in the chapter that follows. These include discussions of how to "do" school, from suggested instructional strategies and techniques for dealing with a multicultural group, to defusing clashes between students from different cultural and language backgrounds.

Values and beliefs are the focus of the sixth chapter. Underlying all aspects of culture and communication are basic beliefs about how the universe unfolds and how individuals should act and interact, even how parts of the body should be held, oriented and moved in given contexts. An appreciation and understanding of the way values and beliefs can mandate what happens in given contexts greatly enhances our ability to work with learners from many cultures.

The final chapter provides practical applications for the ideas, strategies and techniques introduced in the preceding chapters. Questions frequently asked by classroom teachers are identified and answered with concrete suggestions.

The book concludes by listing references for further reading. There are general references for those times when you want to extend your knowledge in areas related to ESL learners, and specific references related to the questions and answers outlined in the final chapter.

. . . .

SETTING THE STAGE

To study a mixed group of immigrants is in itself a liberal
education.

James S. Woodsworth

Countries wracked by internal political conflict
or at war with others, or in which the aftermath of a war is as
horrendous as the war itself, generate immigrants and
refugees. In addition, many people make the difficult decision
to leave their country of origin for reasons that have more to
do with economics than with politics. For a variety of reasons,
then, people from around the world continue to arrive on the
shores of North America.

The United States and Canada are nations of immigrants,
and have received new immigrants and refugees since their
earliest days. Today, they remain two of the industrialized
nations committed to supporting continued immigration.

Although the expectation in Canada has been that new
arrivals will become part of a multicultural community, or
mosaic, this policy was not clearly articulated until relatively
recently. For years, the Canadian government set the rate of
immigration on an annual basis, often in response to turmoil
in other parts of the world. As a result, the number of people
arriving from year to year tended to fluctuate greatly.

In the early 1990s, however, the federal government created
a five-year immigration plan that provided for the number of
immigrants to grow to 250,000 a year between 1992 and 1995

and to 300,000 annually after that. The goal of this policy is to admit about one per cent of Canada's population a year, provided the country can continue to absorb this number. It should be noted that these figures do not include refugees, as it is impossible to forecast the numbers of people who will choose to seek asylum in a given year.

In the United States, the prevailing philosophy with respect to immigration has always been somewhat different from that in Canada. Immigrants are expected to assimilate into the "melting pot." In 1987, 393,200 immigrants arrived in the United States; by 1991, this figure had increased to 447,200. In recent years, the U.S. has received about a million immigrants a year, a figure that includes an estimated 200,000 illegal migrants. Even when illegal immigrants are included in the total, however, the U.S. continues to take in fewer immigrants as a percentage of its population than, for example, Canada or Australia. Even so, the number of people in the United States who do not speak English as a first language continues to grow. By 2010, Hispanics, for example, are expected to become the largest minority group in the U.S., making up 21 per cent of the population.

Historically, Europe was the source of much of the migration to North America. This was true during the entire colonial period of both Canada and the United States, and was especially pronounced after the two World Wars. In the second half of the 20th century, however, the number of individuals and families arriving from Asia, South America, Central America, Mexico, the Caribbean and the Middle East has increased, often dramatically. It is no longer unusual to find students from Hong Kong, Chile, Korea, Romania and Iraq sitting in the same classroom.

The stated commitment of both the Canadian and American governments to deal with the issue of refugees and "displaced" persons has further increased the flow of people to North America. In 1994, the United Nations High Commissioner for Refugees estimated that the number of refugees and persons of concern worldwide exceeded 19.8 million. Though this number has fluctuated since then, the sad fact is that statistics for 2002 show that there has been little change.

In *Forced Out: The Agony of the Refugee in Our Time*, Carole Kismaric reports that refugees may spend from two to 40 years in camps. The average stay is five years. Commitments to attempt to reduce the total number of people in refugee camps, partly through immigration to North America, mean that many teachers are encountering more students whose cultural and linguistic backgrounds are unfamiliar.

In addition, increasing immigration means that our classrooms are likely to continue welcoming ESL students whose countries of origin are more and more diverse. Some of these countries may be small, but others may be relatively large, though the number of students from a given community within the country may be small. Regardless, we, as teachers, are frequently unprepared for the arrival of students from diverse areas of the world.

These new learners bring with them languages, experiences, learning styles and cultural backgrounds that are unfamiliar. Unlike English, which uses a more or less phonographic writing system, some of their languages use a symbol system as the basis of written communication. Some incorporate a highly stylized tonal system into speech, relying on this to indicate meaning rather than using a different word as English does.

In some cases, schools are enrolling students who have had little or no previous formal schooling, or whose schooling has been seriously interrupted by political strife. In Vancouver, for example, some 17-years-olds have arrived with as little as two to three years of schooling, while others do not perceive that education has any great value for them.

When we welcome these students, we must not forget that there is great diversity within every culture. All the students who arrive from a particular country or with similar cultural backgrounds are not going to exhibit the same traits. We must guard against adopting attitudes based on stereotypes (e.g., all Chinese students work hard and are good at mathematics and science). Stereotypes are exactly that; they do not reflect the reality of our classrooms. Sometimes stereotypical attitudes develop unconsciously, and people remain unaware of their thinking until they are confronted with individuals who do not "conform" to their preconceived image.

As students from a greater number of countries and backgrounds arrive in our classrooms, awareness of differences between groups increases. Some students come from a background where their schooling has been consistent, while the schooling of others has been interrupted or non-existent. One group tends to "speak up" in class while another doesn't. Some need one correct answer, while others can live with a variety of possible answers.

Working with a variety of students with diverse linguistic and learning needs forces us to re-evaluate how we teach and the assumptions we can and cannot make. In short, it forces us out of our relatively comfortable and predictable ways of teaching. This cannot help but heighten our level of anxiety and unease.

At the same time, it is important to remember that students from around the world bring with them complete communication systems, individual differences and rich cultural backgrounds. They are able to function very well in many environments, and the fact that they need assistance with speaking English or adapting to new situations doesn't suggest that they have inherent learning problems. Too often, however, it's assumed that these students are deficient. We've all seen people who talk to ESL learners loudly and with exaggerated slowness.

These students often need nothing more than time to deal with the question or direction, possibly by translating it into their first language, formulating an answer in their first language, and then finding the known or appropriate words to articulate a response in English.

It's also worth remembering that not all ESL learners were born outside North America. Some of the students entering our schools were born in Canada or the United States but learned a language other than English as their first language. They require at least as much attention as, if not more than, ESL speakers from other countries. These students are sometimes caught between two linguistic worlds, starting school without solid literacy skills in either their home language or English.

Despite the differences among them, ESL learners also share a number of traits. These traits reflect values, attitudes, belief systems, hopes, dreams and aspirations that transcend language. The differences appear to surface in the way these commonalities are expressed or acted upon.

One area of commonality among newcomers relates to the adjustment process they go through. Students, parents, peers and teachers must consciously learn to interact and adjust to one another in new ways. Academic, emotional, cultural and social conflicts may arise in school settings.

Since the early 1960s, the phenomenon of "culture shock" has received considerable attention. Simply stated, culture shock encompasses a constellation of feelings and events that occur when we are plunged into an unfamiliar environment in which the signs and signals of interaction that we have internalized and taken for granted are no longer valid or effective.

Because of traumatic past experiences and factors surrounding their forced arrival, refugees often experience a greater degree of culture shock than immigrants, who have elected to immigrate to a new home country. Because of this, refugees often need more time to work through these inner conflicts. It's worth noting, however, that some immigrant children who had no say in their parents' decision to leave their country of origin may feel anger and resentment about the situation in which they now find themselves. They, too, need time and support to work through their feelings and adjust to their new lives.

Over the years, anthropologists and social psychologists have attempted to increase their understanding of culture shock. Many view it as a series of stages through which individuals pass, sometimes slowly, sometimes in fits and starts, and occasionally, not at all. An awareness and understanding of some of the more obvious stages of culture shock will help us, as teachers, work more effectively with these new ESL students.

Stage 1—Optimism, excitement. Refugees and immigrants are filled with hopes for a new life and new opportunities. Excitement and optimism replace the anxiety felt before their arrival. Buoyed by these positive feelings, they believe they can overcome all obstacles and that everything will be fine.

Stage 2—Culture shock. They experience culture shock. The behavioral and value orientation of the host culture is different from their own. Instead of being like everyone else, they are in the minority. Everything is different, from job-seeking methods, language and social practices to the most integral part of their being: their values.

Stage 3—Superficial adjustment. Realizing that changes must be made, they attempt to adjust. These adjustments are only superficial, however, and deep down they still interpret everything in terms of their own frame of reference and their own values and beliefs. Comparisons are made between the way things are done "here" and "at home."

Stage 4—Frustration, depression. They encounter some very real problems, which are often overwhelming. Examples include employment and language problems, family crises and racial discrimination. Students, too, experience setbacks in their attempts to fit into the educational system. Stress and pressure lead to frustration and depression. In many cases, problems cannot be shared because they have no extended family or friends to lend support.

Stage 5—Acceptance of and identification with host culture leading to integration. Over time, the problems sort themselves out. Refugees start to gain a better understanding and appreciation of North American culture. They start to go beyond superficial adjustments to readjust their outlook on life in order to be a part of and fit in with the host culture, without totally giving up their own cultural identity.

Though these descriptors apply particularly to refugees, many immigrants also go through the same stages. Often, the length of time it takes to resolve the issues associated with a particular phase marks the only difference in the way the stages are experienced by the two groups. It is not uncommon for immigrants to take two to five years to go through these adjustment phases, and for refugees to take between five and 10 years.

Taking the time to find out where ESL learners are on the continuum of cultural adjustment and consistently communicating with them enables us to find areas of commonality. In this regard, it is important to acknowledge the intimate relationship between culture and communication. Building a successful learning community requires teachers to recognize and incorporate a knowledge that students respond in classrooms according to cultural norms and mores learned and absorbed from the day they were born.

Culture

Culture is often viewed as the means of passing on values, perceptions, attitudes and behaviors, as well as a reflection of tradition, lifestyle and patterned ways of dealing with the world. It includes unwritten rules for routine as well as rules for work and play. As Edward T. Hall put it in *The Silent Language*: "It is a mold in which we are all cast, and it controls our daily lives in many unsuspected ways."

Though the traditional mandate of teachers of non-English speakers has been to teach the English language while acquainting these learners with aspects of the host culture, it is increasingly recognized that developing an awareness and appreciation of the cultural background of the learners improves their chances of achieving a reasonable measure of success at this task.

For instance, the kind of gestures and language people use to communicate with others is largely determined by culture. In greeting others, people may shake hands, embrace, bow to one another, touch noses, touch the feet of another or salute. All these are valid and valued forms of greeting for specific cultural groups.

Culture is not innate. It is handed down from adult to child, and this transmission takes place in both formal and informal

17

settings, including school and home. The role-playing of young children provides some useful examples. Suppose you are observing the five-year-olds in a Kindergarten class. Watch for examples of social behaviors that illustrate the prevailing mores and value systems. See if boys are "allowed' to be the mother when playing house, or if girls are accepted as firefighters. It may surprise you to note the extent of the societal value systems that these young children have already absorbed.

The word "absorbed" has been used deliberately here because, in many instances, these values have not been specifically taught; rather, they have been observed over time and in a variety of situations. "Correct" behavior has been positively reinforced, and "incorrect" behavior criticized in both overt and subtle ways.

The culture in and of our classrooms relates to both language and behavior. In fact, it is impossible to exclude cultural considerations from our work as teachers. Every day, situations involving cultural differences arise in every classroom. The following chart presents some examples of behavior, typical questions teachers may ask as they interpret the behavior through the filter of their own cultural norms, and other possible explanations:

Behavior	Question	Explanation
Avoiding eye contact	Why won't you look at me when I talk to you? Are you hiding something?	Downcast eyes show respect
Reluctance to help a peer	Why won't you work with another student?	Different ideas about sharing and owning knowledge
Appearing tired or uninterested	Why are you so tired? What time did you go to bed last night? Are you bored?	Learning a language is hard work; self-regulated bedtime may be the norm

Behavior	Question	Explanation
Refusing to eat with peers	Aren't you going to eat your lunch? Did you bring a lunch?	Not used to eating with anyone but family members; worried that their food may provoke ridicule
Reluctance to answer questions	Didn't you study? Don't you know the answer?	Processing takes time; used to a system in which choral answers are the norm

Because every individual brings to his or her new country a wealth of different background experiences, teachers have a multi-faceted task. We must note the differences, acknowledge their validity, create mechanisms to uncover their positive benefits, and incorporate them into our teaching as a way of building bridges among students, and between students and ourselves.

Given the high probability that an increasingly diverse group of ESL learners will continue to enter our classrooms, how do we prepare ourselves for their arrival? Looking at "culture" from differing perspectives is a starting point, and is the focus of the next chapter.

AWARENESS OF CULTURE

Culture is so much an integral part of our life that it is often difficult to realize that there are different, but equally valid, ways of thinking, perceiving and behaving.

Peter Chinn

Our attempts to understand another culture may take many forms—reading about it, viewing travelogues, or visiting or living in it for a period. Is there a best way? Probably not. The method we choose depends, in part, on what we mean when we say "understanding" a culture.

It is our belief that an important route to achieving understanding of another culture begins with developing an awareness of our own culture. It is difficult, however, to step back and examine our culture objectively when we are immersed in it.

The following description of an everyday occurrence in one culture, excerpted from Horace Miner's contribution to *Toward Internationalism: Readings in Cross-Cultural Communication*, illustrates this point:

In the hierarchy of magical practitioners, and below the medicine man in prestige, are specialists whose designation is best translated as "holy mouth men." The Nacirema have an almost pathological horror of and fascination with the mouth, the condition of which is believed to have a supernatural influence on all social relationships. Were it not for the rituals of the mouth, they believe that their teeth would fall out, their gums bleed, their jaws shrink, their friends desert them, and their lovers reject them. They also believe that a strong relationship exists between oral and moral characteristics. For example, there is a ritual ablution of the mouth for children that is supposed to improve their moral fiber. The daily body ritual performed by everyone includes a mouth rite. Despite the fact that these people are so punctilious about care of the mouth, this rite involves a practice which strikes the uninitiated stranger as revolting. It was reported to me that the ritual consists of inserting a small bundle of hog hairs into the mouth, along with certain magical powders, and then moving the bundle in a highly formalized series of gestures.

Readers will recognize that the ritual simply involves brushing the teeth, but this particular presentation highlights the importance of perspective.

We can conduct our own experiments with looking at ordinary situations from another perspective. For instance, how would you begin to describe driving a car to someone who has never seen a car? How would you describe the car itself? To someone who has never been to school, how would you describe the organization of the school day? Or the movement of classes when the bell rings?

The movie *The Gods Must Be Crazy* is a delightful example of the way a particular group reacts to the introduction of a foreign object—in this case, a Coca Cola bottle—that seems to have fallen from the sky. The story recounts people's initial reaction to the bottle, how their treatment of it changes over time, how their interactions with each other begin to shift as a result of the discovery, and their ultimate decision about what to do with it.

In industrialized countries, the Coke bottle would quickly be discarded but the perspective of the group portrayed in the movie was completely different. The bottle was a novelty to be examined and experimented with.

The reactions of the characters in this movie point out how much we assume simply because we have never consciously thought about or questioned certain ingrained thinking or behavior. In many situations, we take certain behavioral expectations for granted until someone in the group appears to contravene the perceived norm.

For instance, rituals such as greetings can be confusing. When a young man named Manjit, for example, arrived at the airport after a long flight and looked around at how people were interacting, he was understandably dismayed. He was used to greeting people with the traditional *namaste*, which involves making a slight bow while pressing together the palms of the hands chest-high in a praying position. What he saw were some people shaking hands, others hugging, and some hugging and kissing.

The questions that might have run through his mind include:

— Is this polite behavior in public?
— Why are different people doing different things?
— What should I be doing?
— How do I know what to do?
— How do I know what's acceptable?

For Manjit, the *namaste* no longer appeared to be the appropriate form of greeting, but he was confused about what was correct.

Ask yourself how you greet various people within your personal and professional spheres? Why? What do these greetings reveal about the extent and depth of various relationships? How have your greeting patterns changed over time? What do you notice about the way(s) in which your students greet each other? What do these various approaches lead you to understand about their relationships?

It's worth noting that we must be careful about assuming that our conclusions are correct.

Another example of a ritual we often take for granted is taking turns. During their early years in school, most North American children are taught that taking turns in a systematic fashion is appropriate, valued and correct. In fact, much time and attention is paid to teaching this behavior, and those who do not learn it quickly are often censured.

What is it about taking turns that makes it so important? What associations are there with taking turns? Courtesy? Order? Organization? Symmetry? Purpose? Power? All these and more? What associations accompany a failure to take turns? Disorganization? Chaos? Inability to control? A poor reflection on the abilities of classroom teachers to maintain order?

We have all been in situations in which another person did not wait to take her or his turn, whether it was while driving or waiting at a grocery-store checkout counter. Feelings such as anger and hostility are often engendered at these times, and our reactions may range from silent resentment to muttering through clenched teeth.

In other countries, taking turns isn't viewed as seriously. Indeed, some people look upon this Western form of courtesy with great dismay, wondering how individuals ever accomplish anything or receive any attention at all by acting in this passive way.

In many cultures, it is perfectly acceptable to push, shove, elbow another, or barge in when seeking attention. Seasoned travelers often have tales of times when they temporarily adopted certain unfamiliar cultural behaviors as survival mechanisms, even though they would never dare to exhibit these same behaviors in North America.

When children from cultures that do not value taking turns arrive in North American classrooms, it is all too easy to form hasty judgments about what these students are like. These judgments reflect one value system, but may show an inadequate understanding and tolerance of the different values and behaviors of other cultural groups.

At the beginning of this chapter, we stated that becoming aware of one's own culture is an important starting point for understanding other cultures. Robert Kohls, former director of international programs at San Francisco State University, created one model to assist with this process. In his work with international visitors to the United States, he outlined what he feels are 13 core American values and juxtaposed them with contrasting orientations that might well be much more representative of other cultural groups. Though his intent was to help foreign students and other visitors understand the how and why of seemingly puzzling American behavior, we have adapted his chart on the following page because it provides a window on the values and perspectives many of us share.

Kohls' chart provides one interesting tool that can help us begin to think about cultural values. It does not suggest that all people in North America—or elsewhere—hold one set of values and not another; rather, each characteristic is meant to be viewed as a continuum. We can use it to identify where we sit on the continuum. It can also be used as a tool to help you determine students' viewpoints and articulate strengths and weaknesses in any context.

Values in the United States	Values in Other Cultures
Personal control over environment, responsibility	Fate, destiny
Change is natural and positive	Stability, tradition, continuity
Time and its control	Human interaction
Equality, fairness	Hierarchy, rank, status
Individualism, in dependence	Group's welfare. dependence
Self-help, initiative	Birthright, inheritance
Competition	Cooperation
Future orientation	Past orientation
Action, work orientation	"Being" orientation
Informality	Formality
Directness, openness, honesty	Indirectness, ritual, "face"
Practicality, efficiency	Idealism, theory
Materialism, acquisitiveness	Spiritualism, detachment

In attempting to understand other cultures, it is important to begin with our own because we can develop greater understanding of our own background and the overt and covert forces that shape it. In other words, there can be a better understanding of self.

For each characteristic mentioned in Kohls' chart, think about where you would locate yourself on the continuum. If you are close to one end and you suspect that students in your class(es) are closer to the other, this may present challenges in terms of how smoothly interaction and, indeed, learning, will occur. The greater a teacher's understanding of his or her self, the better able he or she is to deal with issues relating to culture or, when appropriate, to teach specific aspects of culture. A teacher's awareness can help ESL students function successfully in more than one culture and enrich the understanding of their non-ESL peers.

. . . .

ESL LEARNERS ARE

INDIVIDUALS

To speak another's language without understanding the
culture is to make a fluent fool of oneself.

Edward T. Hall

The metaphor of an iceberg is often used to
illustrate culture. The portion of the iceberg above the water
line, which can be easily seen, includes physical
characteristics, distinctive features of clothing, food, art and,
of course, language. The much larger portion below the water
line, however, includes communication style, values,
perceptions and beliefs. It is these less visible aspects of
culture that define our behavior toward and the way we
communicate with others.

The overriding purpose of this book is to illustrate how
inextricably culture and communication are interwoven. This
chapter will examine some of the surface aspects of the
cultural iceberg, highlighting some of the crucial cultural
variables that relate to who ESL learners are and how this
affects their interactions with other individuals, and with
teachers and fellow learners in particular.

It has been said that culture is communication and
communication is culture. When discussing culture and
communication, we must always keep in mind that we are
dealing with individuals. Though members of any cultural
group share certain culturally influenced behaviors and styles
of interacting, we all have our own idiosyncrasies,

motivations and personal styles. In fact, we all are members of several cultures, not only one. The following example illustrates this:

Matthew is in his 12th year of schooling, attending a special high school program in an upper middle class neighborhood. This program for motivated learners includes enrichment activities that range from participation in nation-wide mathematics competitions and science laboratory work at the nearby university to rock-climbing expeditions and ski-camp retreats.

When we read this, we may form an immediate impression of who this young man is. For example, we may assume that he's fairly bright, comes from a well-to-do family that lives in an urban setting, and has had opportunities many students will never have.

In reality, however, Matthew rides the bus for more than an hour every day to get to school because his family cannot afford to live in the fairly expensive housing near the school. He wears secondhand clothing, has no specialized equipment and works part-time to help support his attendance at this school. He lacks the money to participate in the more exotic activities offered at the school and knows that he needs to win a scholarship if he is to go on to higher education.

To which culture does Matthew belong? Several. He belongs to the middle class of a large urban center. His German mother has influenced his taste in food and music with some ethnic aspects of her culture. He associates with students who, like him, do not live in the school's catchment area and whose socio-economic background may or may not be the same as his. He is a strict vegetarian—placing him in a somewhat trendy cultural group—and aspires to be a music teacher, which exposes him to two more cultural groups, teachers in general and music teachers in particular. Teachers and parents of teenagers will know that Matthew also belongs to a powerful teen cultural group that grown-ups sometimes have difficulty understanding.

The initial, superficial description of Matthew may have led us to make a particular set of assumptions about who he is. As information about his heritage and circumstances was added, it became necessary to reassess, sometimes several times, our picture of him. We are all the products of a variety of influences: our heritage, lifestyle, economic circumstances and age group, to mention a few. Therefore, we all belong to several cultural groups, though not all are necessarily clearly definable and many overlap, at least to some extent.

Think about the many cultural groups to which you belong. In addition to your ethnic heritage, these may include groups based on your gender, your marital status, whether you have siblings, and whether you grew up in or outside a city. Too often, we describe ourselves according to a single definition when the reality is that we are influenced by many factors, including many that are cultural.

Judging students on the basis of the superficial description applied to Matthew is short-sighted and can be quite damaging. Yet this has often been the case. As teachers, we need to be aware of the possible conflicts that might arise when, with the best possible intentions, we encourage student-to-student interactions and foster communicative relationships.

For instance, when a new non-English-speaking student comes into a school, a prudent first step is to find someone else in the school, grade or class who speaks the same first language. This buddy can help the new student become familiar with routines and regulations and ease the transition into the new environment.

While this is a good idea, care must be taken not to make inappropriate assumptions when setting up these liaisons by disregarding particulars of the students' backgrounds that may seriously affect this relationship that has been imposed upon them.

For example, while the new student and the buddy may speak the same first language, there may be little understanding between them on any other level. They could, in fact, come from areas that have been sworn enemies for centuries. At the very least, they are the products of their own unique heritage and the circumstances that have brought them to their present situation.

In addition, their relative social or economic status, factors that are often played down in North American society, may be of vital importance for given individuals and their cultural groups. This, also, may make it difficult for assigned buddies to relate to each other. A child from a wealthy family who has never known hunger or deprivation is unlikely to readily see eye-to-eye with a recent immigrant from a refugee camp or a war-torn country, nor will she or he understand the needs and priorities of someone raised on a subsistence farm. In some cases, the children of subsistence farmers are less likely to have had access to formal schooling than even poor children from cities. Both these groups are unlikely to understand the intense focus often placed on education by well-to-do families.

These three groups of children from three very different social, political and economic backgrounds may all speak the same language, but they will operate at three very different levels within a North American school system. Assign buddies, by all means, but use this strategy with care.

Another factor that must be considered is religion. Both history and the contemporary world abound with examples of strife caused by differences in religious beliefs and practices: from the Crusades to the troubles in Ireland and the continuing struggles between Sikhs and Hindus in India and Christians and Muslims in many parts of the world. Again, new students to the school may speak the same first language but be, metaphorically, worlds apart on religious grounds.

Perhaps the most basic aspect of personal differences is gender. No one would deny that gender plays an important role in defining the way people communicate with each other. Nonetheless, in the typical North American classroom where teachers attempt to treat everyone equally, considerable energy is expended in attempting to erase gender as a contributing factor in communication.

In treating all students equally and encouraging them to do likewise with each other, we may be denying a reality that all the students already "know" as a result of their cultural learning outside the classroom and in the home. As we struggle valiantly to ensure equal access to education and higher education for boys and girls, we are lauded by members of one cultural group. At the same time, we may be disparaged by members of other cultural groups who believe these efforts undermine the principles and gender-based traditions of their way of life.

We may also create discomfort if we attempt to buddy up a new student, for orientation purposes, with a member of the opposite sex. If the new student is female, she may be too embarrassed to ask questions of her male buddy and, if the roles are reversed, the new male student may feel insulted to have been assigned a female guide, common language notwithstanding.

Other conflicts may arise because girls from a number of cultures have stayed home from school to help with younger siblings, or the boys from a particular cultural group may warn girls from the same background—in their first language—to keep quiet in class and make no demands on the teacher's time because such forwardness is considered unseemly.

Through the eyes of a member of the dominant culture in North America, these actions seem to impinge on the rights of the girls. It is important to remember that this conclusion results from viewing the incidents from one cultural perspective only. This particular point was driven home in a recent interview with a young woman from a culture in which arranged marriages are the norm. Most North Americans abhor this lack of freedom of choice on the part of the female.

What the young woman made clear is that, although she understood our desire to have what in her culture is called a "love marriage," she wished to point out the many advantages of an arranged marriage, including her own.

First of all, she said that no one knows you better than your parents—and they are also likely to know a great deal about the husband-to-be. Second, your parents are more likely to think clearly about whether the match will be a good one because they are not involved emotionally as one is when "in love." And finally, she pointed out that there is some room to express personal reactions and opinions when the two betrothed begin to meet formally.

In addition, she cited the high divorce rate in North America as well as the high number of single-parent women living below the poverty line. This is almost unheard of when marriages are arranged. In this situation, women are protected and looked after virtually for life—even if the spouse dies, the woman "belongs" to his extended family and continues to live with them and be part of that group.

This young woman was by no means the downtrodden chattel we tend to envision when we take the stereotypical view of arranged marriages. In fact, she was well educated, knowledgeable and articulate about both her own cultural norms and those of English-speaking society. (This is, incidentally, another instance when education plays a role. The situation of an uneducated woman from a rural village in the same country might be somewhat different. However, the interviewee's points are well taken.)

In North America, the style of dress often tends to minimize gender differences. Unless students attend a school where uniforms are the norm, clothing tends to be very casual and definitely unisex. Both boys and girls wear jeans, T-shirts and runners or a variation on this theme. This style may seem somewhat casual to new immigrant parents, though it is not necessarily a major concern.

Style of dress may, however, become more of a concern in gym classes, one of the few areas in the public school system where some sort of uniform is required, usually shorts, T-shirts and runners. While this dress code has been adopted for a variety of good reasons—freedom of movement, coolness, etc.—it is looked upon with consternation by parents of girls from many cultures.

Changing in front of strangers is bad enough, but the unseemly exposure of the legs—whether classes are co-ed or not—and the expectation that a shower will be taken when the class ends are tantamount to blasphemy. As a result, teachers often receive a continual stream of requests to excuse some girls from participating in gym classes or find that they are simply absent on days when physical education is scheduled.

This apparently simple situation begins to highlight some of the underlying issues that create communication problems.

In many cultures, girls and women customarily dress and interact in extremely modest ways, are usually accompanied by chaperons, and never interact with the opposite sex except in formal settings or in extreme private if they are married.

In the same way that many North American parents would be dismayed if their daughters were asked to bare their breasts in phys. ed. classes, so the parents of girls from a number of cultures are distressed when their daughters are asked to expose their legs. This is a cultural norm that is very different and must be recognized and dealt with appropriately, not ignored.

One physical education teacher dealt with this situation by discussing it with the affected students and arriving at a compromise. It took some talking and learning and risk-taking on the part of both the teacher and students before the issue was finally resolved. In the end, the girls wore sweat pants for phys. ed. and were exempted during the weeks when swimming instruction was given. In fact, they volunteered to help in the library while the rest of the class swam.

Gender, together with age, also plays a vital role in defining teacher-student relationships. Though some measure of respect for elders is taught to North American youth, a healthy skepticism and reasoned questioning of any form of authority is tolerated and, indeed, encouraged. As teachers, we cultivate students' ability to think for themselves on matters of importance while, at the same time, demanding respect for and attention to what we consider important elements of education and curriculum. This rather mixed message has resulted in some problems in our public school system; nevertheless, we tend to value reasoned dissent more than blind obedience.

When students from other cultures enter this milieu, they attempt to interact based on the beliefs and values about education developed in their own cultures. In many cultures, education is, first of all, a privilege that is not to be abused in any way. In these cultures, teachers, as adults and educated individuals, are respected, even revered. It is considered the height of insolence and disrespect to question anything the teacher says or does (see the chapter titled "ESL Learners and Schooling" for further discussion of this issue).

Imagine the confusion of students from this particular background when the teacher almost demands discussion and questioning—and when some students respond by questioning and challenging the teacher's knowledge and authority.

A variety of other factors can also create conflict and misunderstandings. If students' access to formal schooling in their home country has been limited, for instance, teachers may encounter teenaged students who have never attended school of any sort, though this by no means implies that they are "uneducated."

In fact, they may have been forced to survive in extreme circumstances, living by their wits if they were to survive at all. In the same class, there may be students from the same cultural background who have attended school from a very young age. These two groups may have only two things in common: they speak the same first language and they do not speak English.

Simply sharing a language does not ensure smooth communication or indicate like-mindedness among ESL students any more than it does among native English speakers. A number of factors—including gender, religion, historical traditions, age and socio-economic status—can influence an individual's identity. To facilitate communication, teachers must take all these into account.

This is the reality teachers face when we work with students from a wide variety of backgrounds. Students may view the process of education and each other in very different ways from what we might be tempted to assume; yet, they may, at the same time, look to us to help them find their way in the new—and sometimes strange—culture and language in which they find themselves immersed.

If we consider the historical, cultural, socio-economic, age and gender issues involved, it will go a long way toward building a better understanding among cultural groups. However, despite everybody's best intentions and even with a reasonable command of the target language, cultural differences in styles of communication can confound these efforts. Communication beyond language, beyond the actual words spoken, is the topic of the next chapter.

. . . .

ESL LEARNERS AND

COMMUNICATION

> If verbal communication is the pen which spells out details, nonverbal communication provides the surface on which the words are written and against which they must be interpreted.
>
> *Earl Stevick*

For a long time, the conventional wisdom suggested that communicating between cultures simply involved learning the language of the other. As a result, much of language pedagogy was based on the heavily linguistic methods used to train diplomats for foreign service. It is now clear that, while speaking a language certainly paves the way for communication, simply knowing the words is not necessarily enough. Rather, language can serve as a bridge to facilitate a deeper understanding of culture.

With this chapter, we have reached the point where we're ready to delve below the surface of the metaphorical waters mentioned in the previous chapter to examine the hidden portion of the cultural iceberg. This portion refers to the less concrete aspects of culture, which manifest themselves as actions and behaviors. Why, for instance, do male members of some cultural groups hug and kiss when greeting one another in public, while members of another group display no touching behavior of any sort and, in a third, only females exhibit this kind of physical closeness?

Actions—or lack of actions—like this can spark a variety of responses, ranging from mere puzzlement to open hostility. The way people communicate with others is an important element of culture and is governed by communication styles, attitudes, values and belief systems. These aspects of culture are rule-governed and quite explicit, but only to those born and raised in the particular culture.

The most obvious component of communication is language. This book assumes that using language to communicate forms the basis for what goes on in the classroom. In addition, however, the way other forms of communication are used is discussed in some detail because these less obvious aspects illustrate cultural differences that may affect overall communication.

We have divided the discussion of these aspects of communication into three areas: coverbal behavior, nonverbal communication, and values and belief systems. The first two—coverbal behavior and nonverbal communication—will be discussed in this chapter. However, because values and belief systems are the complex basis upon which all other communication is founded, the next chapter will deal exclusively with this aspect of communication.

Keep in mind that this division is useful only for illustrating and clarifying issues. In fact, all three aspects of communication interact in both overt and subtle ways to create a style that is culturally based and grounded in firmly held values and beliefs.

Coverbal Communication

In North America, the coverbal and nonverbal aspects of communication have received considerable attention over the last few decades. Researchers have argued that the verbal component of any single act of communication between members of the same cultural group may comprise as little as seven per cent of the act, while the rest consists of coverbal and nonverbal behavior. Even if this percentage is somewhat extreme, it goes a long way toward explaining why simply knowing a language does not guarantee smooth relationships with people from other cultures.

Coverbal behavior—or paralanguage—includes all aspects of voice modification in speech and vocalizations used in listening. For instance, think about the way you listen to a friend describe an experience. As you're listening, you punctuate the tale with comments such as, "Wow!" "You're kidding!" "Uh huh..." and so on. This is coverbal behavior. It demonstrates that you are listening and following the story closely, reacting emotionally with the speaker.

In some Asian cultures, however, this kind of coverbal feedback does not indicate comprehension. The vocalization, and head nodding that often accompanies it, indicate only that the listener is giving the speaker her or his full attention, as is polite.

As teachers, we tend to interpret this kind of coverbal behavior (especially if it is accompanied by head nodding) as an indication of comprehension. The listener seems to be saying, "Yes, yes, I understand. I get it." In fact, this is often not the case, as we discover later when the students in question demonstrate their lack of understanding of the task at hand.

At this point, we may feel frustrated and somewhat duped by the students who gave every indication, according to familiar norms of behavior, that they understood the task and believed themselves capable of completing it. This is an assumption we must try to avoid.

Our precise coverbal behavior varies with the speaker, the story being told, where the story is being told, and the nature of the relationship between the speaker and the listener. In addition, as indicated previously, coverbal behavior is culture-based. In some cultural groups, extensive coverbal feedback while listening may not be considered appropriate at all, or may depend on the relative status, sex and age of the participants.

When we are speaking, our coverbal behavior involves *how* we say what we say. Take the following sentence, for example:

I wouldn't do that if I were you.

In this sentence, we can change the significance of what we're saying by shifting the emphasis. For example, we could place the emphasis on the two occurrences of "I" as opposed to emphasizing the word "do." In fact, we could go through the entire sentence and, by merely shifting the emphasis point, change the intended (coverbal) message. As teachers, we have all used our voices to communicate something beyond the actual words being said, whether this is to warn, give hints, challenge or remain maddeningly neutral.

Intonation has been studied extensively not only within cultures but also across cultures, particularly with respect to the way misunderstanding intonation patterns can cause miscommunication. This is another example of a situation in which simply knowing the language is not enough to ensure effective communication. John J. Gumperz, a linguistic anthropologist at the University of California at Berkeley, has studied this aspect of coverbal behavior extensively and points out the real problems that can arise. Individuals who, to all intents and purposes, speak the same language but come from different cultural backgrounds can seriously miscommunicate their intentions because their intonation patterns are different.

Another aspect of intonation is tone. Most Asian languages, for example, are tonal languages, which means that the same word uttered in a different tone can convey an entirely different meaning. When we consider that some languages have nine or more tones, this becomes a very complex and important aspect of communication.

In English, tone is used to convey feelings, not to change the meaning of words in the literal sense. We have all heard and used this device in our communication, though sometimes we may not be entirely conscious of doing so. The sentence cited earlier to demonstrate that varying emphasis is an element of coverbal behavior hinted at this use of tone.

Saying, "I wouldn't do that if I were you," with the tonal emphasis on both occurrences of "I" may convey feelings such as censure (You sure are stupid to do that!), a condescending assessment of an action (Some people simply don't know how to do things properly!), or a difference of opinion leading to an alternative suggestion for possible actions. Defining which of these three messages—or which combination of the three—is intended depends on the context, the identity of the participants in the exchange and the nature of their relationship with each other.

Although this use of coverbal behavior is fairly well understood, many do not realize that children who perceive a conflict between the verbal message and the nonverbal or coverbal aspect of the same message interpret the nonverbal message as the truth, the "real" message.

Because children are still learning how to act and interact, they are likely to give the coverbal, as well as the nonverbal, message the worst possible connotation. In other words, instead of interpreting the message in the example as, "I'll help you do this a better way," they are likely to interpret it as, "You're so stupid. You can't do anything right." The implication for eroding the self-esteem of learners is obvious.

For these reasons, we must be very conscious of how we use tone to convey meaning in the classroom. For ESL learners, who are having enough difficulty figuring out what the words themselves mean, interpreting tone adds a hidden level of complexity that makes their task even more difficult.

Nonverbal Communication

Nonverbal communication or behavior is much more than simply "not words." It occurs largely out of conscious awareness and is culture-based. In other words, the way we illustrate our words is specific to our culture and is related to culture-specific values and belief systems.

The power of the nonverbal components of communication cannot be overestimated. At some time or other, everyone has likely walked into a room and known instantly, without hearing any talk or seeing any interaction taking place, that something is amiss. How do we know? Because thousands of minute signals that are below our conscious level of awareness tell us so.

In this situation, we may act upon our unconscious, almost instinctive, knowledge by either withdrawing, if we feel like an intruder or outsider, or by asking what is wrong, if we wish to get involved or help in some way. As teachers, we often encounter the aftermath of incidents like this in the classroom or on the playground. Though nothing is said, the atmosphere is heavy with conflict.

In general, nonverbal communication includes the kind of coverbal behavior outlined previously, as well as kinesics, proxemics, haptics and artifacts, which are explained in the material that follows. Silence and time are also important elements of nonverbal communication. When we present ourselves to others, we combine these elements to convey our feelings and attitudes; we use them to "illustrate" the words we are saying.

KINESICS

Kinesics, a term coined by Ray Birdwhistell, includes all bodily movement—posture, gestures, eye contact and so on—that is an integral part of the communication process. Birdwhistell's minute analysis of body movement pioneered research into this area of nonverbal communication. Our bodily movements can have a lesser or greater impact on communication. It has been said that we cannot *not* communicate in the presence of another.

One subcategory of kinesics is the use of gestures, a familiar part of everyday interaction and one that teachers often rely on. Visualize yourself in your classroom, for example. Johnny is off task and chatting to a friend at the pencil sharpener. You catch his eye, frown slightly, shake your head and point to his seat. If both you and the child are from the dominant North American culture, the message is clear to both of you. Signals like this are part of the daily routine of communication in the classroom.

At the same time, teachers need to be aware that the meaning of signals like this won't necessarily be clear to students from other cultures. For her MA thesis, Sylvia studied a group of three- and four-year-olds whose first language was not English. She determined that many typical gestures used by teachers do not transmit the intended message when they are used in the classroom. Rather, as noted earlier, our nonverbal behavior is culture-based; gestures can be as linguistically different as languages.

In addition, because this research was conducted with pre-schoolers, it is also abundantly clear that nonverbal behavior is learned very early and is, by implication, well entrenched by the time teachers encounter ESL learners in their classrooms.

Perhaps the classic example of gestures being completely misunderstood was related to us by an ESL teacher who had taken her class of teenagers on an outing. In an attempt to call them together in a public place, she used the well-known Western gesture, palm up and curling the fingers towards herself.

To her consternation, a group of them began to disperse rather than move closer. She called them by name while continuing to gesture and saw confusion on their faces. Eventually, they responded to her verbal calls and gathered round.

She had unwittingly given these teens a mixed message. Her words indicated that she wanted them to come closer but her gesture was interpreted as "move away." No wonder they looked confused! Much later, she discovered that the gesture needed to gather this group was palm down while waving the joined fingers, rather than palm up. A simple thing like this can not only cause misunderstanding and confusion, but also create the mistaken perception that the students are being deliberately disobedient.

Miscommunication on the nonverbal level is often more difficult to correct than a spoken *faux pas*. If we don't understand the words, we can ask the speaker to clarify or repeat. It would be extremely odd, however, to ask what someone meant by, for example, frowning, rolling his eyes and suddenly exhaling his breath.

In addition, nonverbal communication often takes place outside our conscious awareness and, as stated earlier, is culture-based. As a result, questioning the nonverbal behavior of a speaker is difficult. In the first place, we get a message beyond the words without being clear about how or why we do so and, in the second place, we are interpreting the nonverbal element of the communication from our own cultural base—our own value and belief system—which has led us to act and interact in a particular way in a given setting.

Before leaving the topic of gestures, two caveats are appropriate. Attempting to learn the appropriate gestures for all the cultures represented in a multicultural classroom is unrealistic. Not only is it a gargantuan task (especially because the clientele may change over the course of the school year), but also the use of gestures is dependent on the context.

For the same reasons, it is a good idea to be cautious about using recipe-like books that purport to enable us to "read a person like a book." For example, scratching the side of the nose has been identified as a demonstration of disbelief in what the speaker is saying. What happens if the listener simply has an itchy nose? Books such as this do not address the context of the interaction and the interpretations given are culture-based.

Furthermore, experience has taught that two very common gestures in Western culture are worth avoiding with ESL students. The first is the circled thumb and forefinger to indicate approval and the second is the raised and crossed index and middle finger to indicate that we are wishing someone good luck. Both these gestures have a variety of meanings in other cultures, most of them seriously negative, slanderous or sexual. For these reasons, it would be prudent to avoid them whenever possible!

Eye contact is another common example of culturally different kinesic behavior that is tied strongly to values and belief systems, which will be discussed in a later chapter. For the moment, it is important to note that Western culture pays very careful attention to eye contact. A listener who is honest and engaged makes frequent, though intermittent, eye contact with the speaker during a conversation. On the other hand, constant eye contact—staring—conveys a completely different message.

For example, teachers tend to feel certain that if a listener refuses to make eye contact she or he is, at the least, not attending or, at worst, guilty as charged. This is a value judgment based on cultural norms of nonverbal behavior in given situations. In many cultures, however, frequent eye contact, particularly between an adult and a younger person, is considered the height of rudeness, if not a show of outright hostility and a challenge to the authority of the adult.

As a result, a student who is behaving in a manner appropriate to her or his culture by keeping eyes to the ground and listening in silence can mistakenly be labeled shifty, guilty, dishonest, disinterested or the like. Who has not heard an exasperated teacher proclaim, "Look at me when I talk to you!"

Clearly, these examples illustrate that it is important for teachers to be careful about assuming that the meaning they attribute to a particular gesture is the same as that of the students. In fact, trying not to make assumptions and, when they are made, checking out the conclusions drawn should be the mandate of teachers wishing to limit miscommunication.

PROXEMICS

Proxemics has to do with the use of personal space, the physical distance we place between ourselves and others. The relative placement of physical objects and the use of physical space on a larger scale is also considered to be an element of proxemics. Edward T. Hall, well-known anthropologist, sees all use of space as culture-based and has written extensively about the differences in the proxemic behavior of people from cultures around the world.

To understand this, picture the layout of your classroom. Where is your desk located and how are students' desks or tables arranged? In rows, in groups, lined up squarely with walls or askew?

Does your desk face the students' desks so that you can observe and supervise them while sitting? Is there room behind your desk for only you or is another chair close at hand so it can be drawn up for chats with students, colleagues or parents? When you confer with students, do you do it at your desk or is there a designated spot in the classroom? Does the location allow for side-by-side rather than face-to-face, across-a-barrier contact?

How have you organized your classroom space and why? Some layouts simply reflect the furniture that is available or the custodian's request for arrangements that allow for efficient cleaning, while others are a reflection of personal style and the importance attached to different activities within the space.

The way your classroom is laid out and the way you create space for interaction in the classroom is, in part, a reflection of your preferences with respect to the size of your own personal space bubble. Some of us need to keep our own space—for example, the desk—inviolable and inaccessible while others freely share this space.

Arrangements such as this are often a nonverbal statement of how physically close individuals are inviting others to come. Obviously, sitting across a large desk from someone is more formal than sitting side by side on the same side of the desk. And sitting in student desks across from or beside each other is more formal than sitting on a couch or in other side-by-side-orientations.

In terms of actual physical contact, those who have taught young children know that some are very physically demonstrative, frequently hugging each other and you, while others appear stand-offish and do not like to be touched. This is a reflection of who they are and how big they prefer their personal space bubble to be.

We all use space to regulate our relationships with others. We can keep people at a distance, both physically and metaphorically, or, alternatively, demonstrate positive feelings by drawing someone closer.

Again, this may or may not be done at a conscious level, but the action—or actions—speaks volumes. Great dissonance can be created when a child from a culture in which displays of physical affection are the norm is repeatedly rebuffed by a teacher who feels her personal space is being violated.

As with all nonverbal communication, proxemic behavior, though governed to an extent by individual preference, is also culture-specific. In fact, the tendency is to react to a perceived invasion of personal space at an almost unconscious level, which can create immediate dissonance and miscom-munication.

In the homes of many native English-speakers, for instance, it is common for children to have their own bedrooms from a very young age. In fact, one of the ways parents signal respect for their children's physical and personal space is by knocking on their bedroom door rather than simply walking in.

In a number of cultures in which physical and personal space are more likely to be shared, the custom of giving children their own rooms is considered cold and unfeeling. Though closer living arrangement may simply reflect economic and space issues, the cultural predisposition toward a physically closer style is also part of the equation.

Finally, it must be noted that proxemic behavior is also related to values and belief systems. Gender, age, setting, relationship and status are key variables of proxemic behavior and will be discussed in a later chapter.

When thinking about proxemics, teachers might consider the following questions:

— What is the size of my personal space bubble? Who can invade it and from whom can I tolerate an infringement of this space? Are age, circumstances or other variables important factors?
— How do I deal with students or colleagues who "invade" my space or step on my metaphorical toes? Do I talk about it or simply grit my teeth; remove myself from the close contact or wait for the person to move away?

These questions are seldom asked but are worthy of consideration. A measure of self-awareness, as discussed earlier, can go a long way toward preventing miscommunication when, rather than if, the issue comes up.

HAPTICS

Haptics refers to all touching behavior, from a light tap on the shoulder to the slap on the bum athletes give each other during competition. Obviously, haptics is closely related to proxemics; it is not possible to touch someone, even inadvertently, if they keep themselves isolated in a large personal space bubble.

In the classroom, however, some 30-odd students and one adult spend many hours in closer proximity than may normally be preferred by individual members of the group. In addition, it is quite common for teachers to touch students, particularly younger ones, to show concern, approval and simple appreciation. This, too, can give rise to cultural conflict and misunderstanding.

Unfortunately, children who feel uncomfortable with this kind of touching often don't express their feelings because they are reluctant to appear to be challenging the authority figure, the teacher. As a result, to save undue stress and discomfort for both the students and ourselves, we should be aware of some of the cultural bases of these behaviors.

In primary classrooms, it is not uncommon for the teacher to hug children, give a pat on the head, shoulder or back, or simply take them firmly by the hand and lead them somewhere. As students grow older, this kind of touching usually becomes less frequent, depending on the individual teacher and student and also on the personal space comfort zone of each. School policy may also affect attitudes toward touching.

However, for people from some cultures, even incidental touching in certain areas such as the head or a handshake between the sexes is perceived to be a personal violation or possibly an insult or threat. A legend about the demise of Captain James Cook, the early explorer, illustrates this point.

Apparently when Cook arrived at the Fiji Islands, he was observed and met by the understandably curious indigenous people. As he landed and approached them, he put out his hand in what he thought was the universal gesture of friendship, the handshake. The gesture was not as universal as he believed. The natives, who had been quite ready to be friendly, interpreted Cook's gesture as threatening and decided to kill him.

Though students in our schools will obviously not go to such extremes, the point is well taken. We must never assume that our interpretation of an action, or lack of action, is the only interpretation possible.

Before we leave the topic of haptics, here are some questions to consider:

— Do I allow myself to be touched? By whom? Under what circumstances?
— Under what conditions would I touch the students and where? Am I sure they understand the purpose and non-verbal meaning of this touch?

Far from wishing to create paranoia, we encourage you to think about this type of communication and consider whether it is clearly understood by everyone.

ARTIFACTS

Artifacts refers to the element of nonverbal communication that we consciously create and manipulate. The physical arrangement of classroom furniture is related to this field, which also includes factors such as the colors on the walls, the pictures displayed, the teacher's clothing choices (clothes and adornments), and how space for different activities or tasks is created. "The clothes make the man" is a saying that may seem passé; nevertheless, what we wear gives a definite impression of who we are, the values we represent and the value we place on our interactions with others.

Clothing, mentioned earlier in relation to the blurring of gender lines in the classroom, is a culturally important factor where the teacher is concerned. Though ESL learners and their parents can learn to adjust to casual clothing for their children, a teacher who displays the same casualness is often harder to get used to. In many cultures, the teacher's status implies formality—in speech, relationships and personal presentation, including dress.

In the eyes of immigrants from many cultures, the message sent by a teacher who dresses and speaks casually may be inappropriate. They may believe that teachers who are friendly with students, encourage them to challenge what is said, do not demand that they stand when they speak in class or call them "sir" or "ma'am" cannot be worthy. If the teacher also dresses quite casually, the negative message is even further reinforced.

In addition, the focal points we choose to set up in our classrooms (reading center, science table, etc.) as well as the time and energy we expend on specific topics of study speak volumes about what we consider valuable learning and, by inference, what we wish students to value.

SILENCE

Silence has to do with the amount of time our sense of what is comfortable allows for non-talking during communication. This is different from nonverbal behavior, which is, of course, not an absence of communication.

The need to fill silence with talk varies greatly among cultural groups. In addition, silence is much more comfortable for relatively longer periods with intimates than it is with strangers. In classrooms, silence is demanded for tasks such as silent reading or writing tests, but in personal interactions, such as questioning students, the "wait time" is expected to be very brief.

Some very interesting studies about the wait-time given when carrying on a conversation, indicate that, for English speakers, it is relatively short—mere seconds or fractions of seconds. As a result, when interacting with a member of a cultural group used to taking longer to reflect on what to say next, native English speakers virtually prevent this person from getting a word in edgewise. We feel compelled to fill the "uncomfortably long" silence with words.

More will be said on this topic in the chapter titled "Values and Beliefs," in which the interpretation of silence in conversation is discussed in relation to the values and belief systems that this use of silence can reflect.

TIME

A cherubic seven-year-old enters a corporate boardroom during a meeting. He wishes to give his executive daddy the contents of his piggy bank in return for spending some time with him, because the boy has always heard his father say that time is money.

This excerpt from a 1980s television commercial reflects a cultural value that considers time a commodity. Though this may be an extreme case, North American culture does generally treat time in this way.

In many other cultures, by contrast, time is simply the right time to do something—this is the time to eat, the time to marry, the time to plant or the time to harvest. Because the way time is used and the degree of attention paid to it are deeply embedded in cultural values and belief systems, this topic will also be discussed in considerably more detail in the chapter titled "Values and Beliefs," as well as in the section of the next chapter that deals with attitudes toward schooling.

A Complex Combination

Clearly, communication involves more than simply uttering words. It is worth repeating that the complex elements of coverbal and nonverbal behavior that accompany our words are interrelated, creating communication scenarios that may baffle or please, disturb or reinforce.

The metaphor of the cultural iceberg will be discussed further when we tackle the values and belief systems, lying metaphorically submerged, that underlie the reason and purpose for particular kinds of communication.

Before we move on to this, however, we need to examine another element of who the learners are by becoming aware of the schooling experiences they may—or may not—bring to our classrooms and how these bear on their ability to function and interact in our schools. This is the topic of the next chapter.

. . . .

ESL LEARNERS AND SCHOOLING

> We must work to create classrooms where there is a discourse of possibility and hope ... where we are much more attentive to using the text of students' lives in our work.
>
> *Enid Lee*

In countries around the world, most schools have one thing in common: they contain a captive audience. Beyond this striking similarity, however, there are enormous differences among school systems—in the way they are organized, the way instruction occurs, and the extent to which they conform to the cultural norms of a given society. This chapter will identify some of the difficulties immigrant students and their families experience when they come together in a new school in a new country.

The processes involved in "doing" school are seldom delineated explicitly and are usually learned over an extended period. No matter where we were educated, most of us have internalized our particular experiences of these processes as part of our concept of attending school. This internalization process began in early childhood through role-playing and continued throughout the rest of our time in schools, colleges and universities.

Learning how to do school, however, is an active process that we, as teachers, begin to recognize when alternative styles of doing school are presented. Zemba, a bright 13-year-old when he arrived in Canada, is a case in point. Zemba rarely brought the correct books to class and seemed to want to protect all his books. He stood when answering a question, often before the teacher had finished asking it, and used paper very sparingly.

Inviting Zemba to tell about his previous schooling experiences enabled us to understand that these had been very different from the Canadian experience. For example, he wasn't used to having his own textbooks, as students shared all available print material in his former school. In addition, he was used to classes of 54 students, seated two or three to a desk.

In his previous school, students were expected to stand when answering a question and he had brought this expectation with him. His haste to answer questions was a learned response to a system in which being recognized and treated as a serious learner by the teacher was extremely important.

Because paper was in very short supply in his former country, it was a respected commodity that was used sparingly, if at all. As a result, Zemba used only the portion that was absolutely necessary and saved the rest.

Being made aware of these differences provided valuable lessons for all the students, and led to lively discussions about appreciating what we take for granted, respecting property, conservation, and identifying a range of appropriate and inappropriate ways to gain attention.

Zemba's story makes it clear that expectations and behaviors associated with schooling are culture-specific. What students do in one environment may not be easily transferred to—or considered appropriate in—another environment. This is also true of instructional strategies, the topic of the following section.

Instructional Strategies

When planning instructional strategies, we need to consider differences in background and culture. In English-speaking Western countries, teachers tend to use a range of strategies that not only incorporate large-group discussions, as well as work in pairs or triads, but also focus on cooperative learning and problem-solving through small-group activities. Though these strategies are used widely, they are not necessarily familiar to, or even considered appropriate by, others.

The case of Taki, a nine-year-old from Japan, illustrates some of the differences and the difficulties caused when a child is required to adapt to a new way of doing things. In Taki's former class of 40, the teacher was the transmitter of information, and the students were expected to collectively "parrot" answers to these questions. Students were assigned desks, which were arranged in rows facing the front of the room. Rote learning and memorization were common, and students answered questions individually only when the teacher specifically asked them to.

Taki, like many others, came from an educational system in which the transmission of information was considered far more important than transactions within it. Focusing on the transmission of information occurs for many reasons: large class sizes; few books or supplies; or a belief that this is a better way to teach and learn. This emphasis on acquiring bits of knowledge or facts is very different from the more North American focus on learning how to learn and learning how to gain access to information for a multiplicity of purposes.

Others believe that the process of acquiring information is at least equal in importance to, if not more important than, the end product. Students who are accustomed to one system often have difficulty adjusting to another and may require specific intervention strategies to help them move from one approach to another.

This was the case with Taki. She needed time and specific instruction to help her identify what was expected of her when working with small groups. Furthermore, she needed her confidence boosted to help her realize that she had contributions to make, as did her peers. While all this was occurring, she was also grappling with the idea that small-group, shared activity was another way of learning.

Cooperative learning, as a system of instructional strategies, is popular and has many advantages. An inherent assumption of cooperative learning strategies, however, is that the participants have similar beliefs about sharing knowledge. This may not necessarily be so.

ESL learners from a variety of backgrounds have been taught to act or respond in the classroom in certain ways. As a result, sharing knowledge may run contrary to all their previous experiences. Sharing may represent a loss of power, influence or privilege, or reflect a loss of competitive spirit. Teachers whose classes include ESL learners need to be aware that all members of the group may not hold the same views on sharing.

In contrast to those who are not used to sharing knowledge, some cultures believe that all knowledge is to be shared. Though this level of sharing may epitomize cooperation within a particular cultural milieu, others may view it as undermining motivation to learn, or even call it cheating.

Another factor, related to participation, is the way students have been taught to learn. Some will have learned how to learn by rote and memory, while others will have observed demonstrations without being required to do anything themselves, except watch closely. In still other cultures, students observe until they are ready to do something correctly by themselves.

In many Western cultures, learning by doing is emphasized and trial-and-error is lauded, not censured, as in some cultures. While learning style, also called cognitive style, is rooted in individual predispositions, culture is an overlay that often results in students' preferring certain approaches.

As a result, it's important for teachers to learn about and reflect on the variety of learning systems represented in the classroom. Which students appear to prefer direct instruction that enables them to memorize information, and which seem to use a trial-and-error approach? Which students blurt out answers or ideas? Which begin to contribute only when they are in smaller groups? On a continuum of approaches to learning, where would each student sit? What do all these variables imply when choosing instructional strategies?

Though these questions are intended to help in classrooms that include ESL learners, they are equally valid in monolingual classrooms. It is not within the purview this book to address learning styles in detail, but references for further reading on this fascinating topic are included in the resources section.

Large-group discussions can help learners identify what they know. In this situation, students who "think with their mouths open"—who blurt out anything that comes to mind—play an important role. While they are jumping in and articulating their responses immediately, they provide time for more hesitant speakers to consolidate what they know or to solidify their knowledge of the English labels associated with the concepts. Individualized attention can be provided when the class is broken into smaller groups, triads or pairs.

Dividing the class into triads, in which each member of the threesome has a specific responsibility, is also a useful way to encourage participation. It also provides opportunities for teachers to learn more about a student's language capabilities and to monitor capacity and growth over time.

Group projects are another excellent way of involving the additional-language learner. Projects that involve using many different skills give ESL learners an opportunity to participate more fully, demonstrating their range of talents and abilities rather than drowning in a sea of words. Focusing on skills and talents rather than language proficiency decreases the pressure to use English in a way that may be beyond their capabilities at this time. Further ideas for working with ESL learners in the classroom are presented in the chapter titled "Putting It All Together."

Cultural Conflicts

In every situation that includes people from differing cultural backgrounds, there are bound to be clashes between the students' first languages and cultures and those of the host culture. The classroom is no exception.

Students and their families expect what happens in the classroom to reflect cultural beliefs about education. In North America, for example, play is considered important because of its potential to facilitate learning. In some other cultures, play is considered meaningless and counter-productive to learning. Parents from these cultural backgrounds may become very upset if they see their children playing rather than "working"—or learning.

North American classrooms also tend to focus on ideas and creative thinking rather than data-driven learning, which emphasizes memorizing facts. Parents from countries where data-driven learning is the accepted norm sometimes have great difficulty understanding the approaches used in their child's new school world. Differing cultural expectations are exemplified in parents' questions about how their child is doing in school. Some may ask, "Is she happy?"; others may ask, "Is he respectful?"; a third group may ask, "Is she doing her best work?"; and a fourth may inquire, "Is he neat and tidy?" Each of these questions tells us something about the family's values and background.

Time is an example of an area of potential conflict. The way we conceptualize time and its use is integral to our cultural attitudes. North Americans, for example, tend to view time as a valued commodity, and strive to "make good use of it." The English language is filled with references to time; it is something to be on, kept, saved, used, spent, lost, gained or even killed. Time spent thinking or daydreaming is often viewed as wasted time or, at least, unproductive time.

People from some other cultural backgrounds neither share nor understand this concept of time. Arriving at school or finishing a task on time can raise questions such as, Whose time—yours or mine? What is so terribly wrong with wanting to take longer to finish the task?

The identification of school time also reveals differences in perceptions. For some, it is from 9 a.m. to 3 p.m., for others it is from 8 a.m. to 4 p.m. or 7 a.m. to 1 p.m. and may include classes on Saturdays. Some students identify school time as time spent in classes, while others include the time spent in extracurricular activities. How many definitions of school time would your students provide? When working with students, find out how they identify time in their lives outside school, and why this is so. The variety of responses may surprise you. Further discussion of concepts of time is found in the following chapter.

A second area of cultural conflict may involve differences in the value accorded the first language as opposed to English. The case of Thi Minh, a student from Vietnam, illustrates this.

Thi Minh would speak English in the classroom when called upon, but would revert to Vietnamese on all other occasions. In fact, she seldom spoke and seemed to think that schooling had little to do with her. Her lack of participation in extracurricular activities also concerned her teachers.

With the assistance of another Vietnamese speaker, they investigated and found that Thi Minh's family expected her to maintain her traditional language and culture so that she would be able to pass on ancient values and traditions. They believed that acculturation would erode her ability to do this. Furthermore, in her village, education was valued for males, but not for females. They also learned that Thi Minh worked after school in her uncle's store and looked after her younger cousins. The demands on her time meant that she could not participate in extracurricular activities.

Developing an awareness of differing cultural values and attitudes helps us understand the factors and forces that shape the lives of students. It would have been easy for Thi Minh's teachers to accept their initial interpretation of Thi Minh's attitudes if they hadn't made the effort to investigate further and learn more about her.

We must understand that we are dealing with a variety of complex and interrelated issues. Adapting to a new society takes time, sometimes generations. Amending some currently held values (obviously some will never change, nor should they) also takes time.

We must also remember the role played by economics in scenarios such as Thi Minh's. For many immigrants, starting life in a new country often means that the skills, abilities, training and aptitudes they have brought with them are undervalued. In their new country, they may be forced to take lower-paying and less skilled and responsible jobs than they are used to. In many families, not only do both parents work, but both also frequently work several jobs in order to survive. For them, this is necessary to lay the foundation for a "better" life.

Another factor related to this scenario and the notion of developing a better life relates to the perception of time discussed earlier. Many families view change and betterment as taking place over several generations or even centuries. North Americans, on the other hand, often have a much greater sense of urgency and want to see advances within a relatively short period.

A third area of conflict that crops up with great regularity relates to homework, and the expectations that accompany it. For many from Asian cultures, for example, mathematics is the most important part of the curriculum because scores in this subject are critical to determining the rank or standing of a school. As a result, only math homework is considered relevant.

People from many cultural groups expect their children to do more work at home than is frequently the norm in North America. If this work is not assigned by the teacher, parents have been known to buy workbooks or other materials and insist that students work through them on a daily basis. Often, the students do not fully understand the content of these materials and end up confused and frustrated.

Many parents also expect that homework will be given daily and will start in the earliest school years. By the time students reach secondary school, they are expected to average three to five hours of homework nightly. This facet of student life in Korea is illustrated by the following excerpt from the writing of a young student named Sarah Kang, who is remembering a friend in her home country:

> Her name is Won Hee. She is 18 years old and in Grade 12 in my old school. She wants to be a reporter. She gets up at 6 in the morning. School starts at 7 a.m. We have seven classes a day and extra study time until 10 p.m. After school, she goes to the library to study. She finishes her homework and prepares for the university entrance exam. She goes home at 1 a.m. and eats and then goes to bed. It is her daily life.

When studying and working hard at school are traits carried over from the home country, what happens to these ESL learners in North America?

During informal conversations, some secondary ESL learners told us that they often spend two to three hours completing homework assignments that might involve one hour's work for a native English speaker. They are checking vocabulary usage, meanings, variations on meanings and spelling, and doing other reference work. Some have quietly added that to get to bed before 2 a.m. is a luxury.

A fourth area of conflict relates to the choices students are asked to make. In many elementary classrooms, for example, learning activities are organized in modules or stations and students are encouraged to choose their starting points. In secondary schools, students' choices may relate to selecting optional or elective courses.

Students coming from some other educational systems have often had little or no experience with making choices like these. They are accustomed to having all their courses prescribed, with rigidly articulated performance expectations. Asking a student to choose a starting point, or one course over another, may generate questions such as: How do I decide? How do I know what's more or less important? What if I choose wrong? How do these courses relate to anything else? How much time do I spend on each? Will I get an A on my report card? When even English-speaking students sometimes find it difficult to make these decisions, imagine how difficult it may be for some ESL learners.

Understanding the dilemmas that we may be creating, even inadvertently, for ESL students is important. Sometimes, we may need to identify strategies that limit the range of choices for these students, at least until they feel more comfortable with the process. Often, it is also useful to have a bilingual speaker available to explain procedures and your teaching style to the students and their families in their first language. Additional questions and concerns can also be dealt with directly at this time.

Inviting parents come to the school to do this, however, raises another area of potential cultural dissonance. In many countries in the world, parents have no involvement with the schools, nor is there an expectation that they will be involved. In fact, parents are often asked to come to the school only when there is a serious problem. This doesn't mean, however, that there isn't support for teachers—quite the contrary! There is solid support for them, but it is expressed in different ways.

In some cultures, the teacher's word is law. This often means that parents don't believe they have the right to question or "interfere with" what goes on at school; difficulties are considered the student's responsibility and are frequently interpreted as a failure to try hard enough.

In other cultures, parents show their respect for teachers by giving them *carte blanche* to do as they see fit. This often includes approval to discipline the student physically. A failure to do homework, for example, might result in a caning from the teacher. This action might be further supported at home by parents who add their own corporal punishment. Incidentally, the fact that corporal punishment is not condoned in North American schools may come as a surprise to some parents and should, therefore, be carefully explained to all parents.

Views about the relationship between school and home are often very different from that which prevails in North America, where parents are considered partners in the education of their children. While this view is desirable and supported by research, it is often extremely difficult for families from some cultural groups to embrace because of differences in cultural conditioning and experiences. It may take a long time before they are comfortable participating at a level that is customary in North America.

To introduce and facilitate parental involvement, teachers may wish to consider providing information sessions in the students' first languages. It may also be helpful to identify community leaders who are prepared to function as networking coordinators for other community members. It's always astonishing to discover just how many people, when they are asked, are prepared to assist with settlement issues for newcomers.

Building Bridges

What do these difficulties and differences mean? They mean that we, as educators, must heighten our level of awareness and recognize that they exist. We must also continually probe and question, never assume, until we have increased our understanding of the various backgrounds the students bring to our classrooms. Although we may have no difficulty acknowledging that the world is shrinking, we need to further our understanding of the implications of this metaphor for our classrooms.

We also have a responsibility to look beyond the obvious difficulties and differences to seek out the similarities. We must strive to identify areas of cross-cultural commonality in order to build bridges for and with ESL learners and their families. These bridges will help us—and the students—adjust to the new realities in which we all find ourselves.

Seeking out similarities and areas of commonality moves us into the arena of values and belief systems. Values and beliefs underlie all aspects of culture and communication, and an appreciation for and understanding of how they can affect what happens in given contexts will greatly enhance our ability to work with learners from many cultures. This is discussed in the next chapter.

. . . .

VALUES AND BELIEFS

The belief that one's own view of reality is the only reality, is the most dangerous of all delusions.

Paul Watzlawick

So far, our discussion has focused on a number of aspects of communication, culture and the individual circumstances that color the actions and interactions of the students with whom we work. In this chapter, we will examine more closely the underlying values and belief systems that, translated into action or inaction, often lie at the root of miscommunication.

The literature on cross-cultural communication abounds with examples of apparently inexplicable communication breakdowns. It also clearly highlights how differences in values and belief systems can affect all aspects of communication. Values and beliefs constitute the bottom portion of the cultural iceberg, the base that underpins all the previously discussed elements of communication and culture.

In *The Silent Language*, Edward T. Hall pointed out that "there is not one aspect of human life that is not touched and altered by culture." Though there is tacit agreement about the truth of this statement, the depth of meaning in these simple words is often seriously underestimated. It relates to the kinds of underlying cultural values and belief systems that sometimes spark people to wonder how anyone could possibly ....

We all have a basic set of principles that guide how we live, how we interact with others and with whom we choose to associate. Within a given cultural group, these principles are often not articulated into a clear focus or creed.

Instead, this underlying set of principles is rather like the control system necessary to run a subway. No one riding the subway really notices or is consciously aware of it until it breaks down. This is an apt metaphor for what happens when intercultural interactions go wrong.

Because our underlying values and belief systems guide much of our approach to daily life, recognizing and understanding them is very important to teachers when working with ESL learners. It is in this area, however, that it is often hardest to step outside oneself and reach out to others because, in doing this, we are trying to override the mostly unconscious patterns that regulate our lives.

All cultural groups have values and belief systems. In fact, many elements of these systems are shared; but many are not—and it is in these areas that the roots of conflict lie. When one's cultural toes are trodden upon, it rankles and affects communication long after any specific incident that could be talked about and dealt with on the spot.

Rather than reacting angrily to or ignoring differences that cause friction, developing some insight into and understanding of the key elements that make up culture at this unconscious level can be helpful. As teachers, the onus is on us, the adults, to step back and take the larger view, consider the underlying motivators that have brought about the misunderstanding, and act appropriately in the best interests of the students. When we do this, our increased level of understanding will prove a balm for our poor bruised toes.

In this chapter, we will use several global constructs to address a number of the cultural motivators that can lead to misunderstandings. These constructs are presented as opposites that can be visualized as two ends of a continuum.

Recognizing where we sit on the continuum in relation to students helps us understand and gain insights into our responses when a particular position seems to be challenged by a miscommunication. It will also help us move forward and take the action necessary to resolve the miscommunication. If you have not already done so, we suggest that you think about and decide where you fit on the continua introduced in the chapter titled "Awareness of Culture." Do the same as you read this chapter. Knowing your own comfort level enables you to deal more effectively with learners who are at different points on the continua.

Assertiveness—Compliance

In English-speaking cultures, we tend to believe in the power of self-help—the ability to make something of ourselves if only we make an effort and work hard. In other words, we believe that we control all the practical aspects of our own fate. Exceptions might be made in cases where there is a genetic handicap or physical disability, though many would deem that these, too, should be wrestled into relative submission.

This basic belief has diverse and immensely complex consequences. It enables us to dismiss and even condemn those who don't "make it," those who are forced to turn to various forms of social assistance or, worse yet, to opt out emotionally by using addictive substances. It also enables many of us to ignore the broken individuals who sleep in parks, stand in lines at soup kitchens or beg at the doors of the stores where those who have made it spend their surplus cash.

In fact, some people are even suspicious of the growing numbers on social-assistance rolls and those who go for help to the ever-increasing numbers of food banks. We hold a nagging belief that if only they had worked harder and spent a little more wisely, they would not be in such a predicament.

Contrast this belief with the attitudes and actions that might be generated by a conviction that our role in society is preordained from birth and that all that befalls us is part and parcel of our inevitable fate while on this earth. If we are born to wealth and status, this is both a birthright and a responsibility; if we are born into desperate poverty, this too is as it should be, and efforts to change what is are looked upon almost as sacrilege.

Though there are certainly those who view the universe unfolding from the perspective of one of these two extremes—fate versus individual control—most people would locate themselves somewhere in between. Our position on the continuum influences many of our actions and interactions with others.

Our notion of the desirability of standing up for ourselves, for example, is influenced by this position. Standing up for ourselves implies asserting our rights as individual human beings in any context. English-speaking cultures have a variety of negative metaphors (e.g., being a pushover or a doormat) to describe those who do not act in accordance with this belief.

"The squeaky wheel gets the grease" is a cliché often used to justify self-assertive behavior. Yet, in some cultures, "the nail that sticks up is pounded down" is considered a more appropriate image. When cooperation and consensus-building are of greatest value, asserting individual needs is considered highly inappropriate because it undermines the harmony of the group.

In English-speaking classrooms, we usually try to balance the need to keep some sense of order with our efforts to create a relatively democratic atmosphere in which individuals can assert themselves. "Groupthink," where everyone is expected to react in unison and act as a collective whole without considering individual needs, is viewed unfavorably in many English-speaking contexts.

Consider how students who have been trained from infancy not to stand out as individuals are likely to react in this setting. They are likely to suffer at the hands of their peers—and teachers—without protest and be distressed when asked to express their own opinions. They literally do not have an opinion until the teacher gives them one. A related issue is the case of the student with obvious artistic talent who has been "programmed" from birth to become a doctor or lawyer, ignoring anything that might make her or him stray from this predetermined path.

As teachers, we may find it frustrating to deal with these students and hard to understand their passive attitudes. It is very easy for us to judge them deficient in some way because, we reason, if they were able to think clearly, then surely they would be able to express their own thoughts.

Furthermore, innate differences in temperament, rather than culture, sometimes incur the same feelings of confusion and frustration. An idealist dealing with someone who is very practical or a spiritually oriented person dealing with a materialistic, acquisitive type—and vice versa—may experience the same feelings.

Finally, the assertiveness-compliance continuum also includes our beliefs about the value of change. English-speaking cultures tend to view change as positive, a chance to flex metaphorical muscles, grow and learn in a process that can be frightening, but also exciting. This attitude contrasts sharply with the belief that stability and order, expressed in the form of centuries-old traditions that are deeply embedded, are supreme values.

We continue to receive into our classrooms many refugee and, in some cases, immigrant children, whose sense of stability and continuity and reliance on traditional ways of life have been seriously disrupted. In many cases, they are unlikely to view change for its own sake in the same positive light we do.

In fact, children raised in English-speaking cultures sometimes resist and resent change but usually, in remarkably short order, they become excited about new possibilities if they are presented in positive and inviting terms. This positive attitude is the basis of our belief system that change is almost universally for the better.

Dominance—Submission

The assertiveness-compliance continuum focuses on the power of the individual to effect change and relates to individual traits and beliefs about innate power with which we may or may not be endowed. Aside from individual, personal biases, culture is considered the major determining factor in deciding where on this continuum individuals feel comfortable.

Firmly linked to the relative power of the individual, however, is the role of the individual in his or her cultural group. The various roles and relationships that are part of existence in a social-cultural group determine where each of us sits on the dominance-submission continuum. In fact, our relative position is often redefined with each separate role we play and relationship we become involved in.

Our most basic roles and attendant relationships relate to gender. The way culture defines male and female roles has major implications for us in the classroom. As indicated earlier, a student's gender can affect attendance, class participation and personal choices or perceived options. The previous chapter highlights some of these issues, including attitudes toward education that depend on a variety of factors, including the sex of the students.

In English-speaking cultures, we have become increasingly ambivalent about how carefully we attend to gender differences. On the one hand, we endorse unisex clothing and hairstyles, while on the other, we set distinctly different standards for girls than for their male peers, especially once they pass puberty. Feminism began as a movement toward the emancipation of and equal rights for women and is now sometimes branded as un-female by groups that advocate "traditional" family lifestyles where the mother is the homemaker and raises the children, while the father goes out to work.

Variations on this ambivalence are also played out in our classrooms. As teachers, we expect equal effort academically from both sexes, but we still catch ourselves accepting perceptions that are based on stereotyping. For instance, girls have been said to do better in reading, languages and humanities while boys are expected to excel in mathematics and the sciences; we are surprised when a girl states she doesn't like reading but merely bemused when the difficulty is in mathematics. Oh well, that's typical, we think. In fact, it is not typical at all. Recent reports indicate that young women are entering the math and science fields at the university level and beyond in far greater numbers than young men.

In the midst of this somewhat mixed effort to create an egalitarian society now sit students from other cultures. For many of them, there is little doubt about their roles, both as students and as members of one sex or the other. In some cultures, females of virtually any age are considered both socially and academically inferior to their male counterparts. Girls must defer to boys in the classroom, must never be too assertive and must modify their tone and form of expression to ensure that it does not reflect negatively on male members of the class.

It's easy to make snap judgments that girls who have been trained to think and act this way are meek and possibly not very bright. They seldom, if ever, volunteer an opinion, are watchful of the impression they are making and defer to male students in discussions and groupwork. In addition, they rarely complain, always speak softly and agree with whatever the majority or the teacher decides. Finally, they often keep their eyes modestly lowered under all circumstances, even if this is misinterpreted by fellow students and teachers alike.

Relationships between the sexes, but with someone older, are equally well regulated and internalized. In the dominant English-speaking cultures, what used to be firm lines of decorum, such as automatically respecting elders, have blurred somewhat. In many other cultures, however, elders are considered the keepers of the knowledge and folklore of the group and are often both the guardians and teachers of the young.

This aspect of culture was driven home very directly by an incident that occurred when one of us was teaching in an isolated community. Things appeared to have gone seriously awry when not one parent showed up for an evening of student-led "show-and-tell" about what had been accomplished during the term.

Aside from feeling alternatively mortified (at what she considered a personal failure) and outraged (because the parents just didn't seem to care), Sylvia was genuinely puzzled. The students seemed to like school and were reliable enough about getting messages home. Furthermore, they had expressed some enthusiasm about the projects they wished to display and explain.

Sylvia had overlooked the situations of the students and the historical context of schooling in the community. In the past, schooling had been seen as a impediment, something that took children away from the "real" learning that happened in the home and the community. As a result, school had a negative connotation for parents, who had never participated more than halfheartedly in its affairs.

Furthermore, most of the students in this particular class did not live with their parents. At an early age, they could choose to be responsible in all matters to a member of their extended family. In many cases, this meant taking up residence with this person until they were grown and chose their own paths.

The individuals selected were often the grandparents or other elders of the community—and they were not at anyone's beck and call, unless they chose to be. To really clinch the embarrassing no-show, many elders did not drive or even have access to a vehicle. Nor did they have a telephone to call and say they couldn't—or wouldn't—come. Given that the notice had not been addressed to them in the first place, could it be assumed that they had received it at all?

Needless to say, this experience taught a valuable, though somewhat painful, lesson. The next reporting period found Sylvia sitting at the feet of many of the caregivers, in their own homes, loaded down with the students' creations.

When exploring the relationship between young people and their elders, it is also important to examine the relationship between students and their teachers.

In most North American school systems, for example, serious efforts have been made to draw more men into teaching the primary grades, where the vast majority of teachers have historically been women. At the same time, there have also been efforts to entice more women to teach at the high school level, especially in math and science, fields that have traditionally been dominated by men.

One of the purposes of these efforts is to provide a variety of role models for students of both sexes and to eliminate the stereotype that women are better nurturers, while men deal better with facts and figures. Depending on how male and female roles are valued in their own cultures, however, students from other countries may or may not buy into this view.

Their reactions to female and male teachers may vary considerably, according to the value their culture places on men and women. In addition, many consider it preferable to learn from someone of the same sex.

The level of respect accorded to those who are older also plays a role in determining attitudes toward teachers. Here again, it is important to examine what we take for granted. In most English-speaking countries, a degree of informality in the teacher-student relationship is fostered. This does not imply that the teacher has no authority, but rather points to the more informal and agreeable way we like to couch the reality of who's actually in charge.

Blurring the lines of status and power, both in schools and in the world at large, subtly demonstrates the firmly held belief in the equality of all, no matter what profession or life work they may have chosen. We are often bemused and even made uncomfortable by students from other cultural groups who are overly obsequious by English-speaking standards, jump to attention at a teacher's approach in the hallway or classroom, or remain extremely respectful and formal in all interactions.

While we may initially feel rather pleased to be teaching in a classroom in which we could hear a pin drop, the attraction of this absence of noise—including activity, laughter and talk—begins to pall in time. Many of us believe that classrooms should be busy, lively and relatively happy places, though it's worth being aware that the definition of a "happy" environment is also culturally based.

This view is not universal, however, and ESL students who arrive expecting to be taught by rote and disciplined severely for minor infractions will find a relatively casual approach difficult to understand. Some of them may think there are no rules at all. They may need to be taught, for example, that there is a big difference between going and sharpening a pencil when appropriate and climbing on bookshelves or browsing through the teacher's desk.

Even in English-speaking societies, there are individuals who feel that everything must be strictly rule-governed, even to the point of thinking that teachers should make them learn. Teachers need to find ways to deal with these differences in perceptions and beliefs.

The way adults relate to other adults in a given culture is also relevant. In English-speaking countries, parents and other significant adults in the students' lives are encouraged to become partners in the educational enterprise. As highlighted previously, however, we can't always count on the willing and active participation of parents or guardians in school activities when dealing with parents from various cultural groups.

Furthermore, when parents do come into contact with teachers and school administrators, cultural differences in nonverbal displays of dominance or submission may become evident. Some familiar scenarios come to mind: the parent who nods and gives coverbal feedback as we provide a survey of the student's activities and progress but who never makes eye contact and doesn't appear to follow up with the at-home support we thought she or he had willingly agreed to; the parent who wants to hear only whether the student is well-behaved and respectful of the teacher, and promises to punish severely even the most minor infractions; the parents who gaze fondly at their offspring while the teacher tries to impress upon them how little motivation the child appears to have; and the parent who wants more homework in math even though the child is already performing well above grade-level.

Unless we're tuned in to the significance of these actions, we may make the mistake of thinking these parents don't care, are too strict with and demanding of their children, or seem to agree to help with follow-up but never do. What has actually happened is that the parents have acted and interacted in culturally appropriate ways, based on their own perceptions of the way these interactions should be conducted. Appearing to agree but not following through, seeming to push too hard, and following culturally defined protocols for eye contact and coverbal feedback reflect the cultural value placed on both education and teachers.

Disclosure—Privacy

If you want to keep your friends, don't discuss religion, politics or sex! This adage highlights values and beliefs that fit on the disclosure-privacy continuum. In every cultural group, some topics are considered too private for discussion even among intimates, let alone friends and acquaintances. While these barriers are becoming highly variable within North American society, most teachers would, for example, still react negatively to being asked by the parent of a student—or the students themselves—how much money they make or what training and qualifications they have. If coverbal behavior (tone) that we're not used to is added to the mix, the potential for mistakenly assuming that the parent or student is challenging the teacher's authority or questioning her teaching ability is enormous.

This happened when one of us was acting as a volunteer tutor for a local assistance organization. The patriarch of an extended family group "examined" her motivation and educational background. Absolutely no offense was intended; he was simply carrying out his duties as patriarch of the family, whose members he sought to protect from real or imagined harm.

That these cultural ways were not hers had not occurred to him. What gave her even more insight into this particular cultural difference was his response to the fact that she was *not* being paid for the tutoring. He simply could not fathom that an individual with the excellent qualifications outlined to him would choose to work for free for any reason.

Teachers should be aware that students or their parents—or both—may ask about very personal matters in the same tone and with the same apparent nonchalance that might be used to inquire about the weather or how much new snow is on the ski hill. Perhaps the best approach is to consider possible deflecting statements in advance because, when on the spot, it is often difficult to remain calm and civil. In addition, consider teaching students about the sorts of queries that are and are not appropriate in the cultural milieu in which they now find themselves.

Another level of the disclosure-privacy continuum relates to the solidarity of the family in relation to individual concerns. Questions about how much money you make are personal, but can be dealt with fairly simply. On the other hand, questions about, for example, the reasons for your divorce or your single marital status are another matter entirely.

In English-speaking societies, rules of decorum—who can ask what and when—govern the appropriateness of questions on matters such as this. For some, these matters remain private whatever the cost, as they refuse opportunities to share the pain and stress with a sympathetic friend. They are matters for family only, even if this means bearing the pain in solitude because it is the family that is in crisis. Others gladly seize chances to share their sorrow in a setting of trust.

The same holds true for members of other cultures. Some are willing to share their trials and tribulations, given a little encouragement, while others consider it almost a personal affront or a serious form of prying when they are offered a sympathetic ear.

Sometimes, as we watch students struggle to make cultural adjustments and learn a new language, we offer our assistance, only to be rebuffed or even ignored. At other times, a student may be immensely relieved to find that someone actually cares and is willing to assist.

As teachers, we must be sensitive to these inner conflicts and make ourselves available when the burden becomes too heavy or ensure that students know who they can go to for help when they are ready. If it is clear that an issue has been successfully dealt with, some form of acknowledgment of the struggle may also be appropriate.

Direct Communication—Indirect Communication

Even when a student does approach us or accept an offer of assistance, we may still find that the interaction leaves us with new levels of miscommunication to puzzle over. Instead of laying the facts and issues before us, she may circumvent the real "problem" or couch it in terms that make it difficult for us to figure out exactly what the main issue is.

Or worse in our hurry-up-and-get-on-with-it society, the student may go into a long and rambling explanation of the history of her arrival in her new country, the difficulty of getting settled and so on, leaving us frustrated and inclined to cut short the conversation because it seems to be going nowhere. This scenario highlights differences in communication style, the focus of the direct-indirect continuum.

English-speaking societies tend to favor the direct approach. If we have a question or favor to ask, especially of someone whose status is perceived as higher than ours, we take minimal time for courteous formalities and get "straight to the point".

In fact, native English-speakers have often been stereotyped by other cultures as "hello, how-are-you, good-bye-and- have-a-nice-day" types who neither care about how the person is truly feeling nor are willing to devote much valuable time to finding out. As for having a nice day, this is considered nothing but a formula, similar to the excessive use of please and thank you. It doesn't really mean anything, and certainly indicates no commitment.

For people from many other cultures, however, this kind of direct, to-the-point approach is considered extremely inappropriate and rude. Their approaches to communication, even when the problem is urgent, may appear to be extremely formal, very indirect and even vague.

This can create problems in a number of settings, such as job interviews, in which the candidate may be perceived to be avoiding answering the questions, or parent-teacher conferences, in which the parents may seem concerned only with being agreeable, rather than truly interested in how their child is faring.

All of us have probably heard stories of the "difficulties" experienced by English-speaking businesspeople who have traveled abroad to create economic and entrepreneurial alliances. "Our" team immediately wants to start negotiating and discussing equitable ways of creating partnerships, while "their" team appears to be stonewalling, more concerned with maintaining harmony among its representatives than with "clinching the deal".

Even the language we use to describe interactions such as this point to the direct and forceful nature of Western approaches. No rudeness or disrespect is intended. Rather, people have been trained not to waste the time of a busy executive or other high-ranking official with what may seem to be frivolities.

In addition, when conflicts do arise, the Western approach to dealing with them tends to be frank and open. We "lay our cards on the table," as it were, viewing alternative responses as needlessly circumspect. If someone has been trained to assume that anyone who doesn't immediately "play it straight" must be hiding something, the seeds of suspicion may be sown.

Related to this issue are the strategies used to try to persuade someone—in a more informal setting than the boardroom—to adopt our point of view. First, the fact that most of us think it is appropriate to try to talk someone into a particular approach or way of doing things speaks volumes. Given that persuasion is acceptable, it is considered quite appropriate to wheedle and cajole to get our own way. Tactics such as these are viewed with suspicion by many cultural groups.

In the classroom, teachers often manage the environment by using persuasive tactics, whether this is to encourage students to try something or to intervene in a conflict in an attempt to create order and a measure of conviviality. We should be aware that approaches such as this may be seen as inappropriate, or even totally incomprehensible, by some students.

In English-speaking cultures, face-to-face interaction is the preferred way of dealing with others. In many other cultures, however, a form of go-between is used in these situations, and the higher the status of the negotiators, the less likely they are to consent to meet face to face. Though face-to-face interaction is the norm in parent-teacher conferences, we need to be conscious that this direct approach may create discomfort. This consciousness can go a long way toward avoiding serious misunderstandings.

A final note on the direct-indirect communication continuum relates to competition and cooperation. Though this issue has been dealt with in relation to schooling, it's raised here in relation to the overall approach to interaction of any sort. If your personal approach is basically conciliatory and cooperative, you are unlikely to be seriously concerned about where your child ranks in the class. Rather, you are more interested in hearing about whether he is cooperative, helpful and gets along with his peers. If, however, you thrive on competition, high marks and excellence in all areas may be very important to you and expected of your offspring as well.

Though these issues are not necessarily culture-based and may be individual and personal, there is an understandable tendency for some immigrant parents to be very concerned about the academic success of their children. Often the parents view schooling as a golden opportunity to improve their socio-economic standing by sheer will and hard work and are very intolerant of children who do not appear to strive as hard as they do themselves.

Because the bias in English-speaking cultures is to encourage children to work hard at school while making sure they have time to play and have fun, a parent who demands that homework be sent home from Kindergarten may come into conflict with the teacher. The teacher's efforts to understand the parents' background and circumstances combined with the parents' efforts to find out about the philosophy of our education system will go a long way toward lessening the misunderstandings that may occur.

Flexible Time—Time As a Commodity

Differing perceptions of time were mentioned briefly in a previous chapter. At this point, a more detailed analysis of culture-specific attitudes toward time is in order. Again, this represents a continuum of approaches, with time counted virtually by the second at one end and time as a very flexible entity over which imposed control is seen as neither necessary nor appropriate at the other.

Time is very important in most English-speaking societies, and tends to be "used up" or budgeted according to fairly rigid conventions. For example, suppose you are late for a luncheon appointment. Lateness of a minute or two requires a polite apology, lateness of several minutes calls for profuse apologies and probably an explanation. If you will be significantly more than 10 minutes late, you are expected to make an effort to call ahead. If it is a business lunch, this protocol is even more important. If it is a job interview, lateness of no more than a few seconds is tolerable—if you wish to be considered for the position.

By contrast, in some cultures the correct time for something important is flexible and elusive, perhaps gauged by unwritten religious or spiritual traditions, the tides, the time of year or the position of the sun. For example, the time to eat may be governed by when a person is hungry, not by a clock on the wall or a wristwatch; the time to plant or harvest may be determined in an equally non-specific way.

People raised in English-speaking cultures, socialized in a hurry-up world view, have run into conflict with societies that do not see time as a commodity that is constantly in danger of being used up. With all the good intentions in the world, for example, this approach has led to some notable agricultural disasters in which experts from English-speaking countries have offered assistance in food production to less industrialized nations. Their failure to trust the folklore of the people to whom the help was offered overrode what turned out to be very accurate predictions of "the right time" to plant or let fields lie fallow.

There is a children's story about a young bull named Ferdinand, who is preoccupied with enjoying nature. Rather than getting on with learning, in his case butting heads with the other young bulls in the field, he prefers to sit under a tree and smell the flowers. Though the theme of this story deals with pacifism and aggression, it also speaks to differences in the concept of time; time to simply *be* as opposed to time to *do*.

Parents in English-speaking countries, particularly in some social circles, literally fill their children's days with things to do—music lessons, craft classes, etc.—until there is little room left for the children to simply *be*. In fact, simply "hanging out" is often considered somewhat suspect, and all too likely to lead to no good. Ironically, a common complaint today is that children do not seem to know how to entertain themselves. Perhaps this is because every waking moment is planned for them or filled with entertainments.

In some cultures, however, the personal interactions—whether these are talking, singing or just sitting—that occur in time that is simply to *be* are considered much more valuable than achieving X by time frame Y. When children from these backgrounds come to our classes, misunderstandings are bound to occur. These students might seem to ignore deadlines for handing in assignments or think getting to school on time is not vital. In addition, their parents could, by our standards, be seriously late for meetings with school officials.

Time is also extremely important when it comes to face-to-face interaction. For example, native English-speakers tend to measure the "wait-time" between speakers in minute particles. While everyone has talked—or, should we say, listened—to someone who never allows the speaker to complete a thought, strict conventions usually govern how we take turns in conversation. What may not be as clear is how the length of the wait-time may vary from culture to culture.

As noted in an earlier chapter, people from a culture in which it's customary to take the time to carefully think through what they want to say require a significantly longer wait-time than those from cultures where everybody seems to talk at once.

In addition, if it is appropriate in a particular culture to have long silences to ponder, gaze or simply be, the protocols of turn taking become even more complex and are often disrupted when those who aren't used to this leap into the conversation prematurely. The comfort level of silence in the presence of others was also discussed in an earlier chapter but deserves a brief reminder here as it is a key element of our day-to-day interactions with students in the classroom.

Imagine yourself guiding a class discussion. The usual few are ready to talk instantly, but many seldom take part actively. It would be easy to conclude that some of those who don't contribute do not understand and that others have not done the reading or homework and are, therefore, unable to participate. It's worth remembering, however, that expressing opinions in class may be completely alien to some of the reluctant participants, who may need time to think about a response because they have never been asked to give an opinion. For students who are used to classrooms in which participation means listening and taking notes, responses to requests to say what they think will not come easily. Even when students have been asked to express an opinion, they may be accustomed to giving a careful response that is the result of much thought.

A final aspect of differing views of time relates to orientation or direction. English-speaking cultures tend to be very future-oriented. We look forward to the future, plan our activities on this basis and strive to accomplish X, Y and Z by some fixed point in the future (when I graduate, when I get a promotion, when I retire, etc.).

Though we don't ignore the lessons of the past, they tend not to be the primary force that motivates us to act in a particular way. This fits well with the learning-by-doing and trial-and-error classroom philosophies that were mentioned in an earlier chapter.

For people from many cultures, this lack of reverence for and adherence to what was done in the past and learned from those experiences is difficult to comprehend. This orientation to the past and what it has to teach us every waking moment needs to be acknowledged and considered when dealing with parents of ESL students. Although they may fully understand that they are now in a new culture and country where there are some different rules of conduct and approaches to teaching and learning, their own orientation may continue to be quite different.

The Core of Our Humanity

In summary, our values and belief systems are at the core of what makes us human. Everything we say and do is motivated at some conscious or unconscious level by what we believe is right and appropriate at a given moment. If what we value and believe is not valued equally by those with whom we interact, it colors both our interactions with them and our feelings about them as individuals.

Unfortunately, these perceptions tend to be judgmental, remain tenaciously constant, deepen with experience, and are highly selective; we tend to see what we have been taught from birth to see. This chapter has attempted to highlight some of the key areas where differences in perceptions can lead to miscommunication. We feel strongly that recognizing our own cultural values and increasing our understanding and awareness that others may perceive these values quite differently will help us in our work with ESL learners from different cultures.

So far, we have considered a variety of specific social, economic and cultural issues that make up the context in which we welcome newly integrated ESL learners to our classrooms. This doesn't, however, cover all the questions that classroom teachers can—and have—asked. Addressing some of these classroom concerns is the topic of the final chapter.

. . . .

PUTTING IT ALL TOGETHER

Lord grant me the serenity to accept the things I cannot
change, the courage to change the things I can, and the
wisdom to know the difference.

Author Unknown

Whatat are the implications of the material in this
book for the busy classroom teacher? If all these elements of
communication are really important, and more and more
students are not members of the dominant English-speaking
culture, does this mean that we are constantly dealing with
miscommunication?

Surely, we teachers cannot be expected to learn all the
nonverbal and cultural aspects of communication of every
cultural group represented in our classrooms. Shouldn't
students from other countries be expected to learn to function
and live in their new culture? Shouldn't the onus be on them to
learn new communication and behavior patterns?
Furthermore, how do we teach nonverbal and cross-cultural
communication and which culture and behavior patterns do
we use as a model? Finally, even if we attempted this, how
could we avoid implying that other patterns of behavior are,
therefore, not good enough?

These are just some of the questions that may have crossed
your mind as you read the previous chapters. In this final
chapter, some of the key issues that confront teachers who
find themselves working with new ESL learners will be
addressed. By posing some commonly asked questions, we

hope to review and highlight the most useful points to consider in your day-to-day dealings with these new members of your class.

Where do I start?

Start with yourself. The skills and experience you bring to the classroom, combined with a willingness to venture into a relatively unfamiliar area of teaching and learning, are your greatest assets. Being yourself will provide a positive model for both the new ESL learners and the rest of the class.

Be aware! In this book, we have tried to highlight some of the complexities of culture and communication. Becoming a sympathetic observer of the new students in your class will enable you to become aware of subtleties of behavior that might otherwise have escaped you. Without this awareness, unfortunate misunderstandings between you and the new ESL students—and among class members—can, and will, occur.

Start with the simple things. If you were new to your school, what places, routines and regulations would you need to be aware of to function effectively? For example, the location of washrooms and the office, gymnasium and library could easily be recorded on a map of the school. The layout of many urban high schools is so complex that even some teachers need a map to find their way around. In addition, routines we take for granted, such as assigning a locker, supplying or buying a lock for it, and using it to store equipment needed for school, may be completely unfamiliar to new students.

In elementary schools, an additional issue must be considered. Most elementary classrooms have a cloakroom that includes small, open cubbyholes for personal possessions such as extra books, lunch kits and the like. North American children learn very early that these cubbies are the property of the students assigned to them. As a result, they don't take things from other students' cubbies or put their own things in them. Yet the cubbies are wide open.

Children from other cultures may not feel that their things are safe in this kind of open space. Some may feel the same way about their desks and carry everything home every day. Obviously, this practice should be discussed with the new students, who may need time to adjust to this new approach, especially if they are refugees who are used to guarding their few possessions for fear of losing them.

Recess and lunchtimes may also be new events for students, especially those in elementary schools. Secondary students are more likely to watch carefully and follow the crowd when figuring out how to behave, but elementary students may need help in a couple of areas. First, young learners may need to be taught that recess is for playing out of doors and for eating a small snack, if appropriate. They may also require explanations, and even demonstrations, of expectations for behavior in the playground and on equipment. Some schools designate specific playground areas for various age groups, and rules may govern when specific groups can use the basketball hoops, swings, adventure playground equipment and so on.

Be helpful, but patient. ESL students require a tremendous amount of assistance in many areas as they begin to learn about new cultural and social roles and expectations. It is important to recognize, however, that the new learners may initially be so overwhelmed that they are unlikely to ask many questions, even when the answers would be very helpful. Consider how exhausting it must be to be totally immersed in a foreign language, expected to figure out the conventions of the new environment into which you have been unceremoniously thrust, and asked to function normally as a student. The wisest approach may be simply to ensure that you are available when these students are able to process more new information.

Perhaps the best possible advice we can give is to suggest you follow the KISS (Keep it simple, silly) principle. The sheer volume of input these new students are subjected to in the first few weeks of school precludes them from absorbing elaborate and detailed explanations. When they are ready to process more information, they will let you know—and you will have avoided repeating yourself and feeling frustrated because they "still don't seem to understand."

What else can I do to help ESL learners adjust to my classroom?

Acknowledge that the adjustment issues are many, real and vary from student to student. ESL learners are attempting to cope simultaneously with the loss of everything known and familiar and the fear and anxiety that any form of change can inspire. For example, your acceptance of the fact that, at first, these learners may be silent and appear relatively unresponsive in the classroom will go a long way toward easing the transitions they are trying to make.

There is a delicate balance, however, between displaying empathy and understanding during an adjustment period and spoon-feeding. As the teacher, you have a responsibility to help new students understand and deal with the expectations of their new school.

Make your expectations clear. Do not assume anything. Policies relating to, for example, school attendance, including punctuality, and expectations about completing assignments may not necessarily be familiar to newcomers. In addition, remember that the ESL learners in our midst are still struggling simply to understand in a new language. Reinforcing oral instructions in writing or in graphic form is often a great help.

Personal planners are becoming a common tool in schools and are used even by young learners. Planners teach the basics of time management and reinforce good work habits, careful planning and self-reliance. A tool like this can help already overloaded ESL learners in two ways: it helps teach them good work habits, and it is a visual reminder of what was said and done in class. Even if the teacher must record the data on the pages at first, students will quickly come to understand the purpose of a planner and begin to fill it out on their own.

As a result of discussions with classroom teachers, especially at the upper intermediate and secondary levels, we drafted the following letter to help newly integrated ESL students understand classroom expectations. You may find it helpful to compose a similar letter for the new ESL learners in your classroom.

Dear (Integrated ESL Student):

I want to help you do your best in my class. Here are some things to do and think about so that you can do your best.

1. Write clearly so that I can understand.
2. I know that the way you pronounce words in English won't be perfect, but I want to understand, so please help me by SPEAKING slowly and clearly.
3. I will try not to speak too quickly. LISTEN carefully. Make sure you know <u>what</u> homework is assigned, <u>when</u> it is to be handed in, and <u>when</u> the next test is going to be.
4. To make sure you have UNDERSTOOD the lesson, talk about it with someone else in the class.
5. Do all the READING necessary for this subject. Some material is hard to understand. Therefore, you may have to read it <u>many times</u> or <u>ask</u> a teacher for help. The more you read, the faster your English will improve and the easier reading will become.
6. ORGANIZE your notes. Have one book or section for each subject. Keep all handouts from your teachers in the order they are given to you. Writing a date on each will help you do this.
7. HAND IN all assignments on the day they are due. Talk to the teacher if you are not finished.
8. Keep a VOCABULARY list of important terms for each subject and learn the meanings as soon as possible. Remember that many English words have more than one meaning.
9. ASK QUESTIONS WHEN YOU DON'T UNDERSTAND. You can do this either in class or after class. I know this is hard, but it is important.

Your teacher

The importance of establishing clear, consistent routines and expectations, as well as the students' continuing need for feed- back and support, cannot be overemphasized. In fact, this kind of clarity and consistency is valuable for everyone in the classroom.

Take time to talk to the entire class about how difficult change and adjustment can be. Teachable moments, such as when someone announces the arrival of a new brother or sister or that a friend has moved away, can become worthwhile springboards to discussion of the event, as well as the ambivalent feelings that may surround it. An in-depth exploration of issues such as these can also be tied to curriculum areas such as literature, guidance and the social sciences.

At the same time, make some of the cultural and communication issues explicit for the entire class. Throughout this book, we have talked about the importance of developing an awareness of the complexities of culture and communication. Not only can English-speaking students benefit from insights into their own patterns of behavior and social interaction, but the ESL learners will also benefit. Their own "way of being" will be validated, and they will gain an awareness of culturally appropriate ways to interact in the English-speaking context.

What can I do to include the ESL learners in classroom academic learning activities?

Research in the field of second language acquisition tells us that it takes from two to nine years to achieve academic norms in the second language that are consistent with the students' age and academic level. Given this long time frame, providing support for the ESL learners in your classroom is clearly a long-term commitment. Here are a few suggestions for providing the kind of continuing assistance they need if they are to reach their academic potential in this new language.

— Clearly state—and write out—your expectations. For assignments and projects, ensure that ESL learners have seen a model of what is expected and have been given clear, step-by-step instructions—both oral and written.
— Use learning partners, buddies and teacher-selected groups.
— Give extra time for ESL students to formulate oral answers but don't let them off the hook; expect that they

will speak, given the time to develop a response. Their receptive skills (the ability to understand most of what's going on) will develop much more quickly than their productive skills (the ability to talk about what has been learned or understood).

— Give extra time for assignments and allow for draft submissions to you or a buddy or peer tutor. At first, you may also wish to consider varying the length and complexity of assignments, as well as the kind of responses expected.

— Be encouraging, both verbally and nonverbally (see examples in the chapter titled "ESL Learners and Communication").

— If the objective of a lesson is to ensure that students understand content, evaluate their speaking and writing for ideas, not grammar. For example, a poorly constructed paragraph that nonetheless demonstrates comprehension of the concept deserves a passing grade. On the other hand, if your focus is on grammar, the same paragraph would be viewed in quite a different light.

It's worth noting that teaching grammar for grammar's sake has repeatedly proven to be a poor vehicle for promoting efficient language learning. An emphasis on content-based language learning, on the other hand, has been shown to be highly successful. This holds true even for those new to the English language.

— Give praise and marks for effort, enthusiasm, participation, etc., not only for "perfection." Remember, however, that members of some cultural groups find any form of praise very discomfiting. Noting students' reaction to praise can provide an important guide for future interactions.

— When possible, say a student's name before asking the question and keep others on task by encouraging them to be responsible for helping, paraphrasing, etc.

— Use graphic organizers (e.g., tables, charts, diagrams), as well as visual and concrete materials in your presentations and encourage students to use them in their own work.

— Get to know the students and use them as resources. They come to your classroom with considerable background knowledge that is relevant and useful.

— Provide preparation material, reading lists, etc. at the outset of a new topic or unit of study. Encouraging ESL learners to pre-read new material will facilitate their comprehension and encourage them to participate more in class.

— Distinguish between "teach" and "test."

— Use journal responses to help students synthesize what has been learned and to assist you in finding out what needs more emphasis, teaching, reviewing, etc.

When considering these suggestions, it's important to keep in mind the effect of culture on the way students and teachers interact. The chart on the following page provides a useful overview of cultural issues that may affect this.

For purposes of illustration, the chart pairs common practices in North American classrooms with a somewhat artificial opposite extreme. As explained in the chapter titled "Values and Beliefs," the point on the continuum where each of us feels comfortable is a matter of personal style overlaid with cultural norms.

Teacher Behavior and Expectations	
North American	*Other Possibilities*
Praise is overt.	Praise is embarrassing.
Eye contact is expected.	Eye contact is rude.
Physical contact is normal, especially with younger children.	Physical contact is taboo, especially between sexes.
Physical distance (personal space bubble) is 40-70 cm (1.5-2.5 ft.).	Physical distance is either much closer or much farther apart.
Silence is never prolonged; an instant answer is expected.	Silence is comfortable and can imply thought.

Teacher Behavior and Expectations	
North American	*Other Possibilities*
Most feelings may be displayed but not necessarily acted upon.	Feelings must be hidden or, in other cases, displayed with gusto.
Intimate topics can be discussed openly (few are very private).	Taboo topics are highly variable and culturally defined.
Punctuality is prized.	Time is flexible.
Relative status is not emphasized.	Status is very important.
Roles are loosely defined.	Role expectations are strict.
Competition is desirable.	Group harmony is desired.
Politeness is routine but lapses occur and are forgiven. "Thank you" is enough.	Politeness and proper conduct are paramount, especially in children. Gifts of thanks are offered and expected.
Education is for everyone.	Education is for males first.

The ESL students in my classroom rarely become involved in extracurricular activities. Because this is part of school life in North America, how can I promote their participation?

Participation—or the lack of it—is often a result of differing cultural values or economic constraints or a combination of the two. When you are dealing with students from a culture that does not believe in the educational value of play, including sports, you cannot expect them to participate immediately or enthusiastically.

In addition, many ESL students must help with family responsibilities, from child minding to working at a part-time job, on a daily basis. Given that they also need to complete school assignments, this may leave little time for extracurricular activities.

Nevertheless, much anecdotal evidence suggests that encouraging ESL learners to participate in extra-curricular activities supports their social, emotional, cultural and linguistic adjustment. The benefits cited by teachers include gaining opportunities to use English to speak and interact outside the classroom, to learn North American norms for team play, and to get physical exercise. Some teachers have also noted that joining the school choir results in a dramatic improvement in pronunciation. Here are some suggestions for promoting ESL students' participation.

participating in aspects of school life that go beyond the classroom yields positive benefits.

— Allow them time to adjust to the idea of extracurricular involvement. During their entire first semester or even year at their new school, ESL learners may be far too busy simply acclimatizing and trying to keep up to consider adding more to their schedules. Once this initial adjustment period is over, they are more likely to be receptive to the idea of becoming involved in other activities.

— Capitalize on ESL students' strengths. Find out about their interests and abilities and encourage them in these directions. For example, many students arrive with well-developed skills in specific sports. A personal introduction to a coach or sponsoring teacher can help foster enthusiasm and participation. Other students may be skilled in areas such as board games. If, for instance, there is a chess club in the school, this may be attractive to some students.

— Buddy up where feasible. Participating in extracurricular activities involves taking a certain amount of risk. Pairing ESL students with a classmate who is also interested in a particular activity can help them overcome their anxiety about taking this risk.

— Sponsor or promote new activities. The interests of ESL learners may provide a catalyst for creating new activities or clubs in the school. If the ESL learners are the experts, it will not only raise their self-esteem but also promote interaction with students throughout the school.

— Help the parents of ESL students understand the value of extracurricular activities. Though the students themselves are a useful starting point, remember that parents need to understand the value of these kinds of activities in order to sanction them and encourage their children to participate. Furthermore, it's always possible that the parents will approve only certain activities and deny their children permission to participate in others for social, economic or cultural reasons.
— Help parents understand that co-curricular activities are also an important aspect of school life. These may include swimming programs, field trips, special camping experiences and some elements of physical education programs such as golf or water sports. Members of some cultures feel that only text-oriented classroom activities are educationally valid. Take time to explain the relationship between these activities and the curriculum to ESL parents.

How do I help the parents of ESL learners become involved in school life?

Parents may be reluctant to participate in their children's education for a number of reasons. These include

— Lack of proficiency in English
— The need for both parents to work, sometimes at more than one job
— Younger family members at home (many mothers would never consider leaving their children with a "stranger")
— Feeling that they have nothing to contribute.
— The idea of parents as partners in education is an alien concept

Though some parents may seem reluctant to become involved, they may, nevertheless, consider education extremely important. In fact, improving their children's access to an excellent education is often an important factor in a family's decision to emigrate. Despite the difficulties we may encounter, we need to encourage parents to become partners in their children's education. Here are some suggested strategies for doing this.

— Begin a consistent flow of communication. School-wide or classroom-based newsletters, translated into students' home languages if possible, help develop parents' awareness of what is happening at school. In addition, regularly sending notes to parents that praise their children's accomplishments, both academic and in other areas, helps establish a positive relationship between teacher and parent.

— Inviting comments and information about how parents would like to be involved can help establish and maintain communication. Providing parents with a checklist of possible options is often a good idea. Encouraging them to participate in various events such as field trips or special celebrations also helps improve their understanding of the new educational milieu.

— Parents are often very willing to help with homework but aren't at all sure how to go about it. To help them help their children with assignments, provide useful and clear information and design assignments that will encourage family discussion and participation.

— Home reading programs have proven very successful for all learners. Research makes it clear that the act of reading aloud with a significant older person enhances reading skills. This holds true even when it is not the target language (i.e., English) that is used.

— Value the home languages. Current research into the way children learn language points to the importance of maintaining and strengthening their proficiency in their home language. Encourage parents to continue to use and develop their children's first language. This may include reading bilingual books and books in the home language, as well as sharing stories, legends and songs.

How can I help the rest of the students develop an understanding of the ESL learners in the class?

Never underestimate the power of the teachable moment. Seizing every opportunity to discuss issues as they arise can benefit the entire class. For example, a news event that is being discussed in class may be interpreted differently as a result of different values and belief systems. Miscommunications, which are bound to occur and may be based on a misunderstanding or simply different approaches to a task, can provide opportunities for everyone to learn and gain insights.

Examine the curriculum for possible theme-based issues. The existing curriculum contains a range of opportunities for examining the larger issues related to immigration, change and adjustment. Studying the changes wrought in your country by waves of immigrants over the past 200 years, for example, can highlight for all students that the current influx of immigrants is not unique and may indeed have a number of benefits.

Explicit teaching of cultural understandings may be useful. Rarely do we think about, let alone teach, specific aspects of our culture. On occasion, there may be a place for highlighting both similarities and differences in the way people from different cultural groups view the world. It is enlightening for both groups of students, English-speaking and ESL, to think consciously about and discuss things they have taken for granted or have assumed to be universal.

An example of this might be asking questions. By responding positively, we encourage children, from a very young age, to ask questions. To students raised in a culture where observation is the norm, asking questions will be a completely new concept. In essence, they will need to learn *how* to ask questions.

How can I possibly teach them all they need to know?

You can't. Determine what is reasonable and offer it in small chunks. This will help you develop reasonable expectations of yourself as well as enable students to assimilate the information as they perceive the need for it. Developing your own perspective on what you can reasonably expect to accomplish will give the ESL learners the time they need without neglecting the needs of the rest of the class.

Ask for help. Students in your class or school, colleagues, resource people in the school and community, as well as parents, can contribute to your work with ESL learners. While the onus may be on you to set up tutoring programs or other approaches, both you and the learners will ultimately benefit greatly.

Listen to the ESL students. A survey of 180 ESL learners in an urban high school asked them to identify what teachers could do to help them as they struggled to cope with content materials in their second language. Their responses included the following:

— Write things, including homework, on the chalkboard.
— Slow down the speed when speaking at length.
— Don't isolate us at the back of the room.
— Ask me to stay for help (I'm too shy to ask).
— Encourage us to be active in class (it helps me get courage).
— Give us easier questions and passages to read orally at first.
— Give us more than one day for homework assignments.
— Review work and write important things on the chalkboard.
— Help us to work in groups.
— Take an interest in me other than just my marks.
— Hand out notes so I can study at home.
— Encourage other students to work with us.
— Have lots of patience.
— Don't judge me by my English.
— Don't treat us like strangers.
— Check to see if I understand.
— Explain difficult vocabulary and give us a vocabulary sheet with meanings (it takes so long to look up so many words).
— Don't insult us when we don't understand.

— Please don't say I'm not listening. I really am.

— Smile.

In addition to providing some useful suggestions and confirming that the students know their own needs, these responses also serve as a poignant reminder that ESL learners have needs that go far beyond acquiring language and learning subject matter.

Practice in basic skills can benefit everyone. Though the ESL learners in your class will need far more practice and specific language-based activities than native English speakers, the opportunity for all students to hone their skills should not be overlooked. In fact, you may find that ESL students develop a superior grasp of underlying grammatical structures. Class-wide skill sessions may actually afford them a rare opportunity to assist their English-speaking peers, instead of the other way around.

A Final Word

The key message of this book may be summed up as "take nothing for granted." Cultural norms accepted in the English-speaking world are not necessarily a reliable measure when interpreting the actions of others or for assuming that our own actions will be understood. Nor can they be used to predict what will happen in a given situation. As teachers, we need to transcend our own subconscious cultural training and see "our" ways of operating and interacting with the world as one approach among many.

This book attempts to increase teachers' awareness of culturally different behavior patterns and how these can affect daily life in the multicultural classroom. Increasing our understanding of these differences does not imply that we must accept them as our own. It does imply, however, that heightened sensitivity to different ways of viewing and interacting with the world will enhance our ability to build bridges between and among the cultural groups in our classrooms.

. . . .

RESOURCES

The following resources are organized into sections. First are general suggestions for resources that have been mentioned in this book or that deal with issues relating to students who are learning English as an additional language. Next are readings related to the specific questions posed in the final chapter, titled "Putting It All Together." Finally comes a brief outline of some our personal favorites. These are tools and resources that we have used and found eminently suitable for a wide range of learners with a wide range of linguistic abilities. We suggest that you browse and find what is most relevant to your needs at the moment and take it one step at a time. Happy reading.

General

Abt-Perkins, Dawn and M. L. Gomez. "A Good Place to Begin: Examining our Personal Perspectives. In *Language Arts*. Vol. 70, no. 3: March 1993.

Ashworth, Mary. *Effective Teachers, Effective Schools: Second Language Teaching in Australia, Canada, England and the United States*. Toronto, Ont.: Pippin Publishing, 2000.

Axtell, Roger E. *Gestures: The Do's and Taboos of Body Language around the World*. New York: John Wiley and Sons, 1997.

Banks, James A. and C.A. McGee Banks. *Multicultural Education: Issues and Perspectives*. 4th ed. New York: John Wiley and Sons, 2002.

Banks, James A. *Multiethnic Education: Theory and Practice*. 3rd ed. Needham Heights, Mass: Allyn & Bacon, 1993.

Cole, Robert W., ed. *Educating Everybody's Children: Diverse Teaching Strategies for Diverse Learners*. Alexandria, Va.: Association for Supervison and Curriculum Development, 1995.

Collier, Virginia P. "Acquiring a Second Language for School." In *Directions in Language and Education*. National Clearinghouse for Bilingual Education. Vol. 1, no. 4: Fall 1995. <www.ncbe.gwu.edu/ncbepubs/directions/o4.htm> N.B. Also by V. Collier (and W. Thomas) is a longitudinal study, published in 1997, of 750,000 students from Kindergarten to Grade 11. Titled "School Effectiveness for Language Minority Students," it can be found at this Web address: <www.ncbe.gwu.edu/ncbepubs/resource/effectiveness/index.htm>

Crowhurst, Marion. *Language and Learning across the Curriculum*. Scarborough, Ont: Allyn & Bacon Canada, 1994.

Dunn, Rita. "Learning Styles of the Multiculturally Diverse." In *Emergency Librarian*. Vol. 20, no. 4: 1993.

Early, Margaret. "Enabling First and Second Language Learners in the Classroom." In *Language Arts*. Vol. 67, no. 6: October 1990.

Genesee, Fred, ed. *Educating Second Language Children: The Whole Child, the Whole Curriculum, the Whole Community*. Cambridge: Cambridge University Press, 1994.

Guild, Pat. "The Culture/Learning Style Connection." In *Educational Leadership*. Vol. 51, no. 8: 1994.

Hall, E. T. *The Silent Language.* Garden City, N.J.: Doubleday, 1977.

Hall, E.T. *The Hidden Dimension.* Garden City, N.J.: Doubleday/Anchor Books, 1966.

Henry, F., C. Tator, W. Mattis, and T. Rees. *The Colour of Democracy: Racism in Canadian Society.* Harcourt Brace, Canada, 2000.

Kaprielian-Churchill, S. and S. Churchill. *The Pulse of the World: Refugees in our Schools.* Toronto: OISE Press, 1994.

Kismaric, C. *Forced Out: The Agony of the Refugee in Our Time.* Toronto: Random House, 1989.

O'Malley, J. Michael and L. Valdez-Pierce. *Authentic Assessment for English Language Learners: Practical Approaches for Teachers* . Addison-Wesley, 1996.

Oxford, Rebecca ed. *Language Learning Strategies around the World: Cross-Cultural Perspectives.* National Foreign Language Center Technical Reports Series. No. 13. University of Hawaii Press, 1997.

Oxford, Rebecca, ed. *Language Learning Motivation: Pathways to the New Century,* and *Patterns of Cultural Identity.* Second Language Teaching and Curriculum Center Technical Report Series, No. 11. University of Hawaii Press, 1996.

Oxford, Rebecca L. *Language Learning Strategies: What Every Teacher Should Know.* Boston, Mass.: Heinle and Heinle, 1990.

Richard-Amato, P.A. & M.A. Snow, eds. *The Multicultural Classroom: Readings for Content-Area Teachers* . White Plains, N.Y.: Longman, 1992.

Scarcella, Robin. *Teaching Language Minority Students in the Multicultural Classroom* . Englewood Cliffs, N.J.: Prentice Hall Regents, 1990.

Staddon, N. *Through the Looking Glass: Discipline vs Abuse—A Multicultural Perspective.* Vancouver, B.C.: British Columbia Institute of Family Violence, 1997.

Teachers of English to Speakers of Other Languages, Inc. *ESL Standards for Pre-K–12 Students*. Alexandria, Va.: TESOL, 1997.

Valdez-Pierce, Lorraine and J. Michael O'Malley. *Performance and Portfolio Assessment for Language Minority Students*. NCBE Program Information Guide Series, Number 9. Spring 1992. <www.ncbe.gwu.edu/ncbepubs/pigs>

Waxler-Morrison, N., J.M. Anderson and E. Richardson, eds. *Cross-Cultural Caring: A Handbook for Health Professionals in Western Canada* . Vancouver, B.C.: UBC Press, 1990.
N.B. An updated version of this very useful book for information about culture and communication is in process.

Putting It All Together

Where do I start?

Ashworth, M. *The First Step on the Longer Path: Becoming an ESL Teacher*. Toronto, Ont.: Pippin Publishing, 1992.

Ashworth, Mary and H. Patricia Wakefield. *Teaching the World's Children: ESL for Ages Three to Seven*. Toronto, Ont.: Pippin Publishing, 1994.

Coelho, Elizabeth. *Teaching and Learning in Multicultural Schools: An Integrated Approach*. Clevedon, England: Multilingual Matters, 1998.

Early, Margaret. "Enabling First and Second Language Learners in the Classroom." In *Language Arts*. Vol. 67, no. 6: October 1990.

Gersten, Russell (1996). "The Double Demands of Teaching English Language Learners." In *Educational Leadership*. Vol. 53, no. 5: February 1996.

Gibbons, Pauline. *Learning to Learn in a Second Language*. Portsmouth, NH: Heinemann, 1993.

Gunderson, Lee. *ESL Literacy Instruction: A Guidebook to Theory and Practice.* Englewood Cliffs, N.J.: Prentice Hall Regents, 1991.

Law, Barbara and M. Eckes. *The More Than Just Surviving Handbook: ESL for Every Classroom Teacher.* 2nd ed. Winnipeg, Man.: Peguis Publishers, 2000.

Meyers, Mary. *Teaching to Diversity: Teaching and Learning in the Multi-Ethnic Classroom.* Toronto, Ont.: Irwin Publishing, 1993.

Ovando, Carlos J., V.P. Collier and M.C. Combs. *Bilingual and ESL Classrooms: Teaching in Multicultural Contexts.* 3rd ed. Boston: McGraw-Hill, 2002.

Piper, Terry. *And Then There Were Two: Children and Second Language Learning.* 2nd ed. Toronto, Ont.: Pippin Publishing, 2001.

Samway, Katharine Davies and D. McKeon. *Myths and Realities: Best Practices for Language Minority Students.* Portsmouth, N.H.: Heinemann, 1999.

What else can I do to help ESL learners adjust to my classroom?

Axtell, Roger E. *Gestures: The Do's and Taboos of Body Language around the World.* New York: John Wiley and Sons, 1997.

Dresser, Norine. *Multicultural Manners: New Rules of Etiquette for a Changing Society.* New York: John Wiley and Sons, 1996.

Early, Margaret and Lee Gunderson. "Linking Home, School and Community Literacy Events." In *TESL CANADA Journal.* Vol. 11, no. 1: 1993.

Educational Leadership. "Whose Culture?" (theme issue). Vol. 49, no. 4: December 1991–January 1992.

Genzel, R. B. and M.G. Cummings. *Culturally Speaking.* 2nd ed. Boston, Mass.: Heinle and Heinle, 1994.

Houston, Merylie Wade. "First Things First: Why Early Childhood Educators Must Support Home Language while Promoting Second Language Development. In *Multiculturalism*. Vol. 14, no. 2–3, 1992.

Samway, Katharine Davies and D. McKeon. *Myths and Realities: Best Practices for Language Minority Students.* Portsmouth, N.H.: Heinemann, 1999.

What can I do to include ESL *learners in classroom academic learning activities?*

Anderson, Valerie and Marsha Roit. "Linking Reading Comprehension Instruction to Language Development for Language Minority Students." In *Elementary School Journal.* Vol. 96, no. 3: 1996.

Black, Howard and Sandra Parks. *Organizing Thinking: Graphic Organizers—Book II.* Midwest Publications—National Center for Teaching and Thinking, 1990.

Boyle, O.F. and S. Peregoy. "Literacy Scaffolds: Strategies for First and Second Language Readers and Writers." In *The Reading Teacher.* Vol. 44, no. 3: 1990.

Brownlie, F., C. Feniak and V. McCarthy. *Promoting Success in Your Classroom: Instruction and Assessment of* ESL *Learners.* Minuteman Press, 2000.

Buehl, D. *Classroom Strategies for Interactive Learning.* 2nd ed. Newark, Del.: International Reading Association, 2001.

Collie, J. and S. Slater. *Literature in the Language Classroom : A Resource Book of Ideas and Activities* . New York, N.Y.: Cambridge University Press, 1988.

Cook, D., ed. *Strategic Learning in the Content Areas.* Madison, Wisc.: Wisconsin Department of Public Instruction, 1990.

Hyerle, David. *Visual Tools for Constructing Knowledge.* Alexandria, Va.: ASCD, 1996.

Coelho, Elizabeth and Lise Winer. *Jigsaw Plus*. Toronto, Ont.: Pippin Publishing, 1998.

Kooy, Mary and Jan Wells. *Reading Response Logs: Inviting Students to Explore Novels, Short Stories, Plays, Poetry and More*. Markham, Ont.: Pembroke Publishers, 1996.

Peitzman, Faye and George Gadda. *With Different Eyes: Insights into Teaching Language Minority Students across the Disciplines*. Don Mills, Ont.: Addison-Wesley, 1994.

Petrick, P.B. "Creative Vocabulary Instruction in the Content Area." In *Journal of Reading*. Vol. 35, no. 6: 1992.

Reyes, M. de la Luz and L.A. Molner. "Instructional Strategies for Second-language Learners in the Content Areas." In *Journal of Reading*. Vol. 35, no. 2: 1991.

Steinberg, J. *Games Language People Play*. 2nd ed. Toronto, Ont.: Pippin Publishing, 1991.

The ESL students in my class rarely become involved in extracurricular activities. Because this is part of school life how can I help promote participation?

Though research into the specific benefits of extracurricular activities for ESL students is just beginning to emerge, here are some articles that make the link.

Carns, A., M. Carns, H. Wooten, L. Jones, P. Raffield and J. Heitkamp, J. "Extracurricular Activities: Are They Beneficial?" In *Texas Counseling Association Journal*. Vol. 23, no. 2: 1995.

Coltin, Lillian. "Enriching Children's Out-of-School Time." *ED 429 737*. Champaign, Ill.: ERIC Clearinghouse on Elementary and Early Childhood Education, 1999.

Silver, A. "Play: A Fundamental Equalizer for ESL Students." In *TESL Canada Journal*. Vol. 16, no. 2: Spring 1999.

Weiler, J. "The Athletic Experiences of Ethnically Diverse Girls." *ERIC/CUE Digest No. 131.* 1998.

How do I help the parents of ESL learners become involved in school life?

Anderson, Jim. "Listening to Parents' Voices: Cross Cultural Perceptions of Learning to Read and to Write." In *Reading Horizons.* Vol. 35, no. 5: 1995.

Finders, M. and C. Lewis. "Why Some Parents Don't Come to School." In *Educational Leadership.* Vol. 51, no. 8: 1994.

Pecoraro, D. and B. Phommasouvanh. *Limited English Proficient (LEP) Parent Involvement Project: Overview and User's Guide.* St. Paul, Minn.: Minnesota State Department of Education, 1991.

Violand-Sanchez, E., C.P. Sutton and H.W. Ware. *Fostering Home School Cooperation: Involving Minority Language Families as Partners in Education.* Washington, D.C.: National Clearinghouse for Bilingual Education, 1991.

How can I help the rest of the students develop an understanding of the ESL learners in the class?

Blanton, L.L. and L. Lee. *Multicultural Workshop: A Reading and Writing Program.* Boston: Heinle and Heinle, 1994.

Corbitt, J. Nathan. *Global Awareness Profile.* Yarmouth, Maine: Intercultural Press, 1998.

Dresser, Norine. *Multicultural Manners: New Rules of Etiquette for a Changing Society.* New York: John Wiley and Sons, 1996.

Fanning, Peter and M. Goh, eds. *Home and Homeland: The Canadian Immigrant Experience.* Addison Wesley, 1993.

Fantini, Alvino E., ed. *New Ways in Teaching Culture.* Alexandria, Va.: TESOL, 1997.

Genzel, R. B. and M.G. Cummings. *Culturally Speaking.* 2nd ed. Boston, Mass.: Heinle and Heinle, 1994.

Jobe, Ron. *Cultural Connections: Using Literature to Explore World Cultures with Children.* Markham, Ont.: Pembroke Publishers, 1993.

Levine, D., J. Baxter and P. McNulty. *The Culture Puzzle.* Englewood Cliffs, N.J.: Prentice Hall, 1987.

Levitan, Seymour, ed. *I'm Not in My Homeland Anymore: Voices of Students in a New Land.* Toronto, Ont.: Pippin Publishing, 1998.

McAloon, N. "The Teachable Moment." In *Journal of Reading.* Vol. 36, no. 2: 1992.

Sawyer, D. and H. Green. *The NESA Activities Handbook for Native and Multicultural Classrooms.* Vancouver, B.C.: Tillicum Library, 1990.

How can I possibly teach them all they need to know?

Students need a combination of academic, cultural and social learning to become comfortable and fluent learners in the school environment. Adjustment and access are key elements for the teacher to consider. We suggest that you browse the previous sections for a book or article that seems to deal with the issue(s) relating to a specific student or group.

Our Personal Favorites

WEB SITES

Here are some reputable Web sites that will help to keep you up-to-date.

<www.culturegram.com>
Though this Web site leads only to information about the CultureGrams series, it is worth exploring. Culturegrams, which are updated and revised annually, represent the best and most recent knowledge about world cultures and are available for about 170 individual countries, as continent "chunks" or as a complete set. These documents, which are available in a paper version or on CD-ROM, are excellent

sources of information for teachers and are also fairly accessible to learners. They support various approaches to studying countries of the world as part of a social studies project, and their clear and repetitive format (e.g., all use the same topic headings) provide an excellent scaffold for selecting sub-topics when teaching research and note-taking skills.

<www.cal.org/crede>
The Centre for Research on Education, Diversity and Excellence provides information about four kinds of continuing projects: two-way immersion programs, newcomers' language and acquisition, school community programs and sheltered instruction.

<www.cal.org>
The Web site of the Centre for Applied Lingustics is the gateway to vast amounts of information related to ESL issues beyond that covered on the Web site of the Centre for Research on Education, Diversity and Excellence.

The Web site of the National Clearinghouse for English Language Acquisition and Language Instruction Education Programs provides many worthwhile links, including Online Library, In the Classroom, Language and Education, Databases, etc. To help decide where to go, try clicking on What's New, or go to Ask NCELA to check out the most recent research.

<www.ascd.org>
Though the Association for Supervision and Curriculum Development deals with more than ESL, it has produced many very fine publications that are pertinent to our work with ESL learners in a multi-ethnic classroom setting. A little searching always turns up useful tidbits. Try clicking on News and Issues, then Education News.

<www.crosscultured.com>
CrossCultural Developmental Education Services, which is based in Washington State, provides presentations and

workshops, as well as useful products. Two of its notable publications are *Cognitive Learning Strategies for Diverse Learners* and *Separating Difference from Disability: Assessing Diverse Learners.*

Once ESL students can make their basic needs and wants known, both orally and in writing, classroom teachers must try to include them in learning as much of the curriculum as possible. This presents a huge challenge, for both the teacher and ESL learners. We have found the following strategies particularly useful because they scaffold learning for students with a wide range of abilities.

READER RESPONSE

Reading to students models good pronunciation and a love of reading and storytelling. Additionally, these stories can be used to illustrate concepts and teach history and the norms and values of different cultures. Start with picture books—the variety and range of topics today is staggering—and move to short stories, chapter books and novels as appropriate.

Keeping a response journal is an invaluable tool. Even if they include invented spellings, odd phrasings and gaps, simple response journals provide you with information about students, from their mastery of grammar and vocabulary to their comprehension of concepts.

Helping all students see life from someone else's perspective is also a worthy goal. When new ESL learners join a class, your efforts to do this can be of immense value both to the class as a whole and to the newest learners in it. Picture books are a good starting point, and short stories and novels are the logical next step. Whenever possible, give students be given their own copies of the text as this further enhances their learning and comprehension.

Though many novels feature immigrant protagonists and some may even be required reading at various grade levels in your jurisdiction, we have used the following short-story collections with great success.

Levitan, Seymour, ed. *I'm Not in My Homeland Anymore: Voices of Students in a New Land.* Toronto, Ont.: Pippin Publishing, 1998.
This collection of (very short) stories written by immigrant and refugee adolescents appeals to a wide range of learners and provides wonderful support for discussion and writing.

Fleischman, Paul. *Seedfolks.* New York: HarperCollins, 1997.
Thirteen people of all ages and backgrounds write from thirteen perspectives about an empty, garbage-filled lot that is gradually turned into a community garden in the heart of the city.

GRAPHIC ORGANIZERS

Large expanses of text are difficult for many learners to comprehend, and ESL students are no exception. Graphic organizers can help in note taking, make introducing new concepts more comprehensible and help organize all kinds of information. Research has shown that students of many cultures and language backgrounds are exposed to common ways of organizing knowledge, such as Venn diagrams and classification trees and cycles. Because the classification of animals, for example, involves a great deal of vocabulary, drawing a classification tree shows underlying relationships and enables the new learners to concentrate on learning the words. Teachers who try to help ESL learners by creating graphic organizers often find that the rest of the class demands copies of these visuals, which help them clarify their notes and remember constructs.

BUILDING CROSS-CULTURAL UNDERSTANDING

Though novels and picture books can help build understanding and empathy, they may not fit a particular curriculum. Sometimes, a more direct approach is appropriate. Many simulations and role-plays are available and much has been written about cross-cultural communication and understanding. Several titles of interest are included in the references.

MORE TITLES FROM THE PIPPIN TEACHER'S LIBRARY

Helping Teachers Put Theory into Practice

STORYWORLDS
Linking Minds and Imaginations through Literature

MARLENE ASSELIN, NADINE PELLAND, JON SHAPIRO

Using literature to create rich opportunities for learning.

WRITING PORTFOLIOS
A Bridge from Teaching to Assessment

SANDRA MURPHY, MARY ANN SMITH

*How portfolios can help students become active partners
in the writing process.*

SUPPORTING STRUGGLING READERS

BARBARA J. WALKER

*Building on struggling readers' strengths to help them broaden
their strategies for making sense of text.*

ORAL LANGUAGE FOR TODAY'S CLASSROOM

CLAIRE STAAB

*Integrating speaking and listening to help children
discover the power of language.*

THE PHONOLOGY FACTOR
Creating Balance with Beginning Readers

NADINE PEDRON

*How phonological awareness skills can be integrated
into literature-based, meaning-centered classrooms.*

AN EXCHANGE OF GIFTS
A Storyteller's Handbook

MARION V. RALSTON

*Imaginative activities to enhance language programs
by promoting classroom storytelling.*

LIFEWRITING
Learning through Personal Narrative

SYDNEY BUTLER, ROY BENTLEY

Helping students see themselves as writers.

INFOTEXT
Reading and Learning

KAREN M. FEATHERS

Classroom-tested techniques for helping students overcome the reading problems presented by informational texts.

WRITING IN THE MIDDLE YEARS

MARION CROWHURST

Suggestions for organizing a writing workshop approach in the classroom.

LITERACY ACTIVITIES
FOR BUILDING CLASSROOM COMMUNITIES

ARDITH DAVIS COLE

A former "ditto queen" explains how she substituted creative activities for boring, repetitive seatwork.

INQUIRY IN THE CLASSROOM
Creating It, Encouraging It, Enjoying It

DAVID WRAY

How careful planning can ensure that projects become a driving force in students' learning during the early school years.

IN ROLE
Teaching and Learning Dramatically

PATRICK VERRIOUR

A leading drama educator demonstrates how drama can be used to integrate learning across the curriculum.

LINKING MATHEMATICS AND LANGUAGE
Practical Classroom Activities

RICHARD McCALLUM, ROBERT WHITLOW

Practical, holistic ideas for linking language — both reading and writing — and mathematics.

THE MONDAY MORNING GUIDE TO COMPREHENSION

LEE GUNDERSON

Strategies for encouraging students to interact with, rather than react to, the information they read.

LANGUAGE, LITERACY AND CHILDREN WITH SPECIAL NEEDS

SALLY ROGOW

How primary teachers can support children with special needs, ensuring that they are able to truly participate in mainstream classrooms.

KEYS TO LITERACY FOR PUPILS AT RISK

LEE DOBSON, MARIETTA HURST

Building on the strengths of youngsters at risk of missing out on literacy.

AN ENGLISH TEACHER'S SURVIVAL GUIDE
Reaching and Teaching Adolescents

JUDY S. RICHARDSON

The story of an education professor who returns to a high school classroom determined to put theory into practice.

THOUGHTFUL TEACHERS, THOUGHTFUL LEARNERS
A Guide to Helping Adolescents Think Critically

NORMAN UNRAU

How teachers in all disciplines can use listening, talking, questioning, reading and writing to help students become thoughtful learners.

FUSING SCIENCE WITH LITERATURE
Strategies and Lessons for Classroom Success

CARYN M. KING, PEG SUDOL

Step-by-step lesson plans for integrating literature and science with 9- to 11-year-olds.

THE FIRST STEP ON THE LONGER PATH
Becoming an ESL Teacher

MARY ASHWORTH

Practical ideas for helping children who are learning English as a second language.

TEACHING THE WORLD'S CHILDREN

MARY ASHWORTH, H. PATRICIA WAKEFIELD

How early childhood educators and primary teachers can help non-English-speaking youngsters use — and learn — English.

LEARNING TOGETHER IN THE MULTICULTURAL CLASSROOM

ELIZABETH COELHO

Practical ideas for making groupwork work in a multicultural context.

USING STUDENT-CENTERED METHODS WITH TEACHER-CENTERED ESL STUDENTS

MARILYN LEWIS

How teachers can help ESL students become independent learners.

LINKING LANGUAGE AND THE ENVIRONMENT
Greening the ESL Classroom

GEORGE M JACOBS, PRAMARANEE M KUMARSAMY, PAYOMRAT NOPPARAT, SUAN AMY

Integrating language instruction and environmental education.

THROUGH OTHER EYES
Developing Empathy and Multicultural perspectives in the Social Studies

JOAN SKOLNICK, NANCY DULBERT, THEA MAESTRE

Strategies and plans for helping students understand the perspectives of others in historically authentic and developmentally appropriate ways.

AND THEN THERE WERE TWO
Children and Second Language Learning

TERRY PIPER

Practical resource for helping children achieve proficiency in English.

IS THAT RIGHT?
Critical Thinking and the Social World of the Young Learner

IAN WRIGHT

A rich source of inspiration for promoting the use of thinking skills throughout the school curriculum.

PARTNERSHIPS IN LEARNING
Teaching ESL to Adults

JULIA ROBINSON, MARY SELMAN

A wealth of strategies for developing rewarding partnerships with students, colleagues, institutions and communities by employing a collaborative approach that focuses on the learners.